THOUGHT PATTERNS FOR A SUCCESSFUL CAREER®
Mastering the Attitude of Success™

THE
PACIFIC
INSTITUTE®
6800-520V2-0615

ABOUT THOUGHT PATTERNS FOR A SUCCESSFUL CAREER®
Mastering the Attitude of Success™

The foundation of all human action is human thought. Our thought process forms the foundation on which we build every facet of our lives. Therefore, it is important for each of us to understand how our minds work – how we got the habits and attitudes, the beliefs that may stand in the way of releasing our vast inner potential and leading fulfilling and purposeful lives. Our beliefs and expectations about ourselves, our families, our organizations – indeed, our world – are directly reflected in our "performance reality."

Thought Patterns for a Successful Career® is designed to build your understanding, with a structured process, of how your mind works, and how you can control the way you think to achieve success – in any part of your life that you desire. Based on decades of research in the fields of cognitive psychology, social learning theory, and high achievement, the education presented here stands at the forefront, reflecting the qualities and characteristics of high-performance individuals and organizations.

Vividly presenting the concepts and education on video, this program provides revealing and productive insights into how you think and how your thoughts affect how you act. The tools and techniques being taught, by easily recognizable stories and examples, can be applied immediately to help you reach your goals easily and enjoyably. Life is propelled out of the ordinary and into an exciting adventure.

By your participation in this program, you join millions upon millions of people around the world who have discovered that the path to true success lies in their own thinking. From small business proprietors to Fortune 1000 executives; from clergy to the military; from educators to political leaders, the economically disadvantaged and prison inmates; from students to bureaucrats, athletes, healthcare professionals and high-tech industries – all are using this information, this education, to make a positive difference in the world around them.

ABOUT THE PACIFIC INSTITUTE®, LLC

The Pacific Institute was founded by Lou and Diane Tice in 1971. Since then, the company has expanded onto six continents and into over 60 countries, and its programs have been translated into a multitude of languages. It has developed a reputation for offering the most practical and enlightening programs ever to come out of the fields of cognitive and self-image psychology, social learning theory, and high-achiever research. International headquarters for The Pacific Institute is in Seattle, Washington.

The guiding principle of The Pacific Institute is that individuals have a virtually unlimited capacity for growth, change and creativity, and can adapt readily to the tremendous changes taking place in this fast-paced, technological age. Central to this is that individuals are responsible for their own actions, and can regulate their behavior through a structured process that includes goal-setting, self-reflection and self-evaluation, among other things.

By applying The Pacific Institute's education, people are able to develop their potential by changing their habits, attitudes, beliefs and expectations. This, in turn, allows individuals in an organizational setting to achieve higher levels of growth and productivity, as well as shifting the collective behavior. This shift leads to more constructive organizational cultures and healthier, higher-performing workplaces.

Solidly grounded in the latest research coming out of the fields of cognitive psychology and social learning theory, documented results clearly show measurable increases in organizational effectiveness and productivity after applying The Pacific Institute concepts.

ABOUT LOU TICE

 He may have started out as a high school teacher and football coach, but a belief in "no limits" led Lou Tice to become one of the most highly respected educators in the world. His singular style of teaching – taking the complex concepts and current research results from the fields of cognitive psychology and social learning theory, and making them easy to understand and even easier to use – brought him students from all over the globe.

The Pacific Institute believes that excellence is a process – an achievable, continuous process that inevitably results when we learn to control how we think, what we expect and what we believe. International business, political and military leaders consult with The Institute on how to do more with less and bring out the best in those with whom they work. Top athletes master the psychological aspects of peak performance. Educators have learned strategies that motivate both staff and students to set and achieve meaningful goals.

Lou's ability as a consummate teacher and mentor brought him to some of the world's hot spots: to the leaders of Northern Ireland, where he worked since the mid-'80's; to Guatemala, since the signing of the Peace Accords in 1995; and to South Africa, from before the end of the era of apartheid. In 2004, he brought his considerable talents to bear in an ongoing partnership with then-University of Southern California head football coach, Pete Carroll, to make a positive difference in South Los Angeles.

Born and raised in Seattle, Washington where Diane, his wife, still makes her home, Lou received his bachelor's degree from Seattle University. He went on to earn an MA in Education from the University of Washington, with a major focus in the mental health sciences. Lou is the internationally recognized author of the popular books *Smart Talk for Achieving Your Potential* and *Personal Coaching for Results*.

In the final analysis, Lou Tice was a masterful teacher and educator whose education is remarkably successful at empowering individuals to achieve their full potential.

ABOUT DR. JOE PACE

 Dr. Joe Pace is a nationally known speaker who conducts seminars and workshops in areas of school management, faculty development, student retention, psychology, and motivation. He has instructed thousands of college-level students in the areas of psychology, personal development, and business administration.

He has earned a Doctorate in Education, a Master's degree in psychological counseling, and a Bachelor's degree in business administration. His doctoral dissertation and over 30 years of research – concerning success concepts and innovative student retention and persistence techniques – have led him to lecture internationally and to pen many articles in his areas of expertise.

Dr. Pace, psychologist and former college president, currently serves as the Managing Partner of the Education Initiative for The Pacific Institute. He is the creator of the *Success Strategies for Effective Colleges and Schools* program, which has been implemented internationally by The Pacific Institute. He is also an educational and psychological consultant for various schools, colleges and organizations throughout the United States and Canada.

From 1974 to 1988, Dr. Pace was Chairman of the Board and President of Prospect Hall College in Hollywood, Florida. Before joining Prospect Hall College, he was the Director at Fort Lauderdale University; prior to relocating to Florida, he served as the Director of Jamestown Business College in Jamestown, New York.

Dr. Pace was appointed, by the Governor of Florida, to the Florida State Department of Education's nine-member licensing commission for private schools, serving on the commission for 10 years, and elected chairman twice. Additionally, he is a former president of the Florida Association of Postsecondary Schools and Colleges.

On a national level, Dr. Pace served as Commissioner of the Accrediting Council for Independent Colleges and Schools in Washington, DC. He served on the Executive Committee of the Council and also on the Board of Directors of the Association of Independent Colleges and Schools (currently known as the Career College Association CCA).

ABOUT DR. SCOTT FITZGIBBON

 Dr. Scott Fitzgibbon has been involved in career education since 1991 with wide-ranging experience in academics, admissions, student services, and career services. Scott has worked extensively with school administrators and faculty specializing in cognitive-behavioral training directed toward affecting employee and student persistence and retention. He has taught thousands of employees and students to apply behavioral understanding to teaching, learning, teamwork, customer service, and sales.

Dr. Fitzgibbon has been a Master Facilitator of The Pacific Institute's *Investment In Excellence®* and *Thought Patterns for a Successful Career®* programs since 1995. Working with The Pacific Institute Higher Education Initiative, this student success curriculum has been implemented in over 500 career schools across North America reaching over 1,000,000 students and 35,000 school employees.

In addition to his work within education, Dr. Fitzgibbon has designed and implemented professional development training and evaluation initiatives for healthcare and service providers, social service and government agencies, and manufacturing. He has earned a Doctorate in Education Administration, a Master's degree in Student Personnel Services and Counseling, and a Bachelors degree in Business Finance. He is a Licensed Professional Counselor.

Dr. Fitzgibbon has guest lectured for numerous international, national and state association conferences.

USING THIS MANUAL

Your Participant Manual is designed and written to supplement the video program. This investment is in yourself, and the manual is designed to support, enhance and expand those excellent qualities you already possess. Your active participation will cause a wealth of effective, practical, self-educating concepts to come alive for you.

The Participant Manual is used to capture your insights, which includes, for each unit, an overview of the concepts being presented, learning objectives, learning principle, key concepts, personal and professional reflective questions and video summary.

The reflective questions in each unit are designed for just that – reflection. As the Greek philosopher Plato once said, "The unexamined life is not worth living." This course gives you time to think about what you think about – something most of us don't take the time to do. The reflective questions will help you see how the concepts can apply immediately to the way you run your life, your family, your team or organization.

Notes pages are provided for you to record your thoughts and insights. As you watch the video segments or read the Summaries, or from your classroom discussions, ideas and discoveries will flow to the surface. It is helpful to capture these thoughts. In the hustle and bustle of everyday life, it is too easy to rush past these insights, so date your entries.

You are urged to not view this manual as a work designed for passive reading. It is a guide for your personal fulfillment and future purpose. Like you, it is a work in progress.

THOUGHT PATTERNS FOR A SUCCESSFUL CAREER®
Mastering the Attitude of Success™ • Participant Manual
©The Pacific Institute®, LLC

ACKNOWLEDGMENTS

PROGRAM DEVELOPMENT

Lou Tice, M.A. Education

Joseph Pace, Ed.D.

Scott Fitzgibbon, Ed.D.

CURRICULUM ADVISOR

Diane Tice, B.A. Education

VIDEO PRODUCTION AND EDITING

Christy A. Watson

Arlys Lopez

Josh Hnosko

WRITTEN TEXT AND EDITING

Christy A. Watson

Scott Fitzgibbon, Ed.D.

LAYOUT AND DESIGN

Courtney Cook Hopp

Special thanks to Mike Seifert for his help in the production of this program.

TABLE OF CONTENTS

TABLE OF CONTENTS

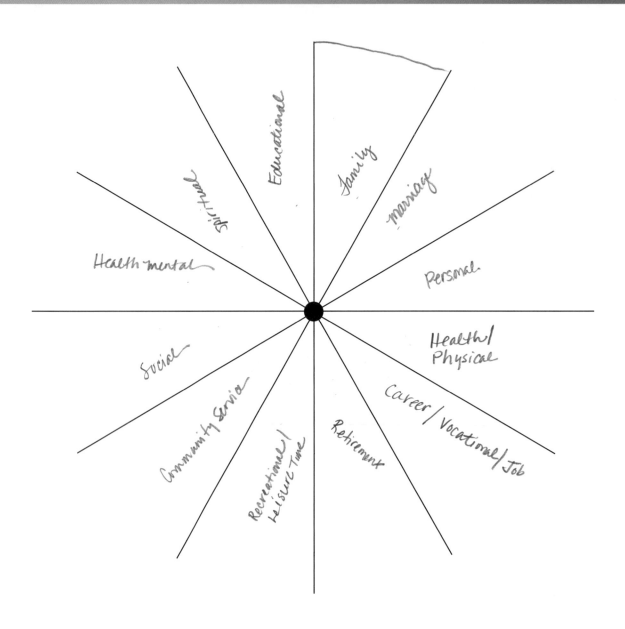

- Personal ✗
- Family ✓
- Health/Physical ✗
- Health/Mental
- Spiritual ✓
- Social ✓
- Career/Vocation/Job ✓
- Retirement ✗
- Marriage ✗
- Educational ✗
- Recreational/Leisure Time
- Community Services ✗

THOUGHT PATTERNS FOR A SUCCESSFUL CAREER®
Mastering the Attitude of Success™ • Participant Manual
©The Pacific Institute®, LLC

THOUGHT PATTERNS FOR A SUCCESSFUL CAREER®
Mastering the Attitude of Success™

SECTION 1: CONTEXT FOR THE COURSE

UNIT 1

The Introduction to The Pacific Institute® will provide you with insight into the worldwide use of The Pacific Institute's curriculum.

UNIT 2

As the co-founder of The Pacific Institute, and mentor to both Dr. Pace and Dr. Fitzgibbon, Lou Tice challenged those around him to answer simple questions before beginning any endeavor: "So what?" "Who cares?" and "What difference does it make?" In this unit's video segments, we set up the purpose and intent for the curriculum you are to receive by answering the Why, What, How and Who questions of its importance to both your academics and your career.

Why, What, How, and *Who.* These units have been established so you will better understand:

*   *Why* this course is important to both your education and career;

*   *What* you should get out of your participation in the course;

*   *How* the content will be delivered; and

*   *Who* will benefit from your participation in the curriculum.

UNIT 3: OUT OF ORDER – INTO ORDER

This segment offers insights into how you can use this curriculum to help you stay in school, complete your education and graduate. You discover that your mind already has many of the tools you need to succeed; you just need to activate them.

Context for the Course: INTRODUCTION

A MESSAGE FROM THE PACIFIC INSTITUTE

The course you are about to take is grounded in the latest research from the fields of cognitive psychology and social learning theory. The core curriculum has been implemented in nearly one third of all the countries in the world, in a variety of languages. *This program has been created for you to use to help take you wherever you want to go in your education, career, and life.*

Dr. Joe Pace, Chairman of The Pacific Institute's Education Initiative, has been involved in Higher Education for over 40 years, holding titles as president of colleges and educational associations. Dr. Scott Fitzgibbon's background is in designing and implementing training (ranging from healthcare and related service providers, to social service and government agencies, insurance and manufacturing), as well as being a licensed professional counselor. These backgrounds have been integral to the process of creating this specific program for you.

The Pacific Institute itself has a five-decade track record of providing its education to over 60% of the current Fortune 1000 companies throughout the world, as well as to corrections and law enforcement, healthcare providers, government agencies, as well as athletes and athletic teams (amateur and professional). In education alone, over 1.5 million students have participated in curricula offered by the Institute.

Why do all these organizations use The Pacific Institute's curriculum? To optimize the release of human potential; build people and organizations that intentionally set, assimilate, and migrate toward their goals; and to create cultural and organizational character that attracts both customers and employees.

Why is the curriculum used in education? Because student retention matters. For students who do not succeed in education, it is rarely because of aptitude or the inability to do the work to get the diploma, certification, or degree. Rather, it is because of the failure to navigate the obstacles, the rocks in road, between the start of education and completion.

It is not a matter of "I can't," or "I'm not capable." It is the commitment and accountability toward the goals you set. It is the process of assimilating that goal which produces the drive, energy, problem-solving to make it happen. By deliberately learning how the mind works and applying that knowledge toward adjusting habits, attitudes, and beliefs, in pursuit of your goal, you will release your potential in both your education and your career. Best of all, it's not magic.

The education you are about to receive is the best of what science and psychology have to offer as far as insights into how we can use our brain most effectively. It is the application of the information that allows you to release the potential inside. After every concept in this course, we encourage you to reflect, to apply, and to practice, practice, practice.

It is our sincere hope that you see The Pacific Institute's curriculum as not just an academic course but rather as one of the world's most widely used *professional development* programs brought into your education. As Lou Tice, our founder, used to say, "Always keep in mind, it's not what you know, but what *you can use* of what you know that makes all the difference."

2 Context for the Course: WHY?

OVERVIEW

"Why am I taking this course?" It's a fair question to ask. As students, we want to know that what we are learning is going to pay off for us down the road. We are investing in our futures and everything needs to count toward the goal of graduation and getting the career we want. This can be a stressful time in life. But, what if it doesn't have to be? What if we can find a way to reduce the stress, uncover past obstacles to our success, and streamline our thinking to ease the way? That's what this course is all about.

OBJECTIVES

By the end of this unit, I will understand:

- the importance of self-discipline, as I begin my college education.

- grittiness is a personal asset as I look at each course on my schedule.

- how willpower helps me grow into my goals.

Set your goal, and grow into it.

LouTice

KEY CONCEPTS

Assimilate/Assimilation: The incorporating of an idea or thought into the subconscious; the absorption or process of incorporating something external into one's body or cognitive processes; making new visions a part of our lives; e.g., one learns and can behaviorally manifest mastery of fundamental mathematical processes.

Goal(s): A sought end that may be actual and objective, or internal, subjective and operational; conceived future; distal goals are end-results, targets; proximal goals are near-term means to the end-result.

Goal-Setting: The act of establishing what we want.

Habit: A learned act; a pattern of activity that has, through repetition, become automatic, fixed, and easily and effortlessly carried out.

THOUGHT PATTERNS FOR A SUCCESSFUL CAREER®
Mastering the Attitude of Success™ • Participant Manual
©The Pacific Institute®, LLC

NOTES

Write down your ideas, observations and insights as you work through this unit. Date your entries.

Will Power :

REFLECTIVE QUESTIONS

1. In order to graduate, I need self-discipline with these particular tasks (Example: attendance, studying, homework):

2. I need to rely on my grit when faced with these obstacles or courses that lie along my path to graduation:

3. What is the strongest, most important image for me to hold, providing all the willpower necessary to drive me to graduation?

THOUGHT PATTERNS FOR A SUCCESSFUL CAREER®
Mastering the Attitude of Success™ • Participant Manual
©The Pacific Institute®, LLC

SUMMARY

WHY is The Pacific Institute curriculum and this course important in setting up your education?

- In a University of Pennsylvania study, "Self-discipline predicted academic performance more robustly than did IQ. Self-discipline also predicted which students would improve their grades over the course of the school year, whereas IQ did not." Their conclusion verified that self-discipline has a bigger effect on academic performance than does intellectual talent. [Duhigg, Charles, *The Power of Habit: Why We Do What We Do in Life and Business* (pages 131]

- In a study conducted at West Point, researchers found that grittiness – which they defined as the tendency to work strenuously toward challenges, maintaining effort and interest over years despite failure, adversity, and plateaus in progress, rather than IQ or standardized test scores – is the most accurate predictor of college grades. [Duhigg, Charles, *The Power of Habit: Why We Do What We Do in Life and Business* (pages 123-124]

- With more than 137,000 current employees and more than one million alumni, Starbucks is one of the nation's largest educators. At the core of their education is willpower. They have identified it as the cornerstone habit for individual success. [Duhigg, Charles, *The Power of Habit: Why We Do What We Do in Life and Business* (pages 131-132]

It is rarely, if ever, that students do not succeed because they don't have the aptitude, or capability of learning the material. Rather it is because they lack:

- the self-discipline to attend classes or log-in daily, turn in the assignments when due, or make studying a daily habit;

- the grit to keep going during tough times like juggling finances while going to school, handling family obligations, relying on various or inconvenient modes of transportation, experiencing technical difficulties, balancing childcare, and possibly lacking a strong support group;

- or the willpower when faced with a subject you don't particularly enjoy, a teacher that's not the greatest, or other students who are distracting rather than cooperative partners in education;

- Or just the willpower to get what needs to be done, when "I just don't feel like it at this moment."

When you assimilate the goal of completing your education, you will learn how characteristics like self-discipline, grit, and will-power are a natural by-product of deliberately and intentionally growing yourself into your goals.

Self Discipline / Grittiness / Will Power

NOTES

....

....

....

....

....

....

....

....

....

....

....

....

....

....

....

....

....

....

THOUGHT PATTERNS FOR A SUCCESSFUL CAREER®
Mastering the Attitude of Success™ • Participant Manual
©The Pacific Institute®, LLC

2 Context for the Course: WHAT?

OVERVIEW

"What results should I expect from this course?" We can expect to get mental technology that will serve us in everything we do from this point onward in life. The courses we will take to obtain the careers we want typically cover the hard skills we will need to succeed with prospective employers. However, the one thing that powers up those hard skills will be the way we think. And in this course, we learn how to think effectively to help us get where we want to go.

OBJECTIVES

By the end of this unit, I will understand:

- that intellect can only take me so far along my career path.

- the value that soft skills – self-awareness and relationship skills – bring to an employer.

- each of these soft skills are easily learned and applied to all aspects of my life.

*Self-reflection is not selfish;
it is necessary for continuous growth
toward who we want to be.*

LouTice

KEY CONCEPTS

Belief(s): An emotional acceptance of a proposition, statement, or doctrine.

Goal(s): A sought end that may be actual and objective, or internal, subjective and operational; conceived future; distal goals are end-results, targets; proximal goals are near-term means to the end-result.

Self-Regulation: Adhering to and following an internal standard.

THOUGHT PATTERNS FOR A SUCCESSFUL CAREER®
Mastering the Attitude of Success™ • Participant Manual
©The Pacific Institute®, LLC

NOTES

Write down your ideas, observations and insights as you work through this unit. Date your entries.

REFLECTIVE QUESTIONS

1. These are the "hard skills" that I am required to have, in order to reach my career goal:

2. These are the "top 10 soft skills" that I believe I need to have, in order to maximize my opportunities for career success:

SUMMARY

WHAT result should you expect from the understanding and application of this curriculum? Albert Einstein cautioned, *"We should take care not to make the intellect our God. It has, of course, powerful muscles, but no personality. It cannot lead. It can only serve."*

Researchers and authors Daniel Goleman, Richard Boyatzis, and Annie McKee analyzed data from close to 500 competence models from global companies (including IBM, Lucent, PepsiCo, British Airways, and Credit Suisse-First Boston), as well as from healthcare organizations, academic institutions, government agencies, and even a religious order, to determine which personal capabilities drove outstanding performance within these organizations.

They then grouped capabilities into three categories:

1. Purely technical skills such as accounting or business planning

2. Cognitive abilities such as analytic reasoning

3. Traits showing emotional intelligence, such as self-awareness and relationship skills

Their findings – the "rule of thumb" as they call it – hold that emotional intelligence (EQ) contributes 80% to 90% of the competencies that distinguish outstanding from average. [Goleman, Boyatzis, McKee (2013) *Primal Leadership: Unleashing the Power of Emotional Intelligence*]

Your academic institution has made the commitment to help you develop hard skills (technical skills that are necessary for your chosen career path) but also (and more importantly) the soft skills (EQ/Emotional Intelligence) necessary for both the completion of your education and to maximize your success within your career.

Emotional intelligence is based on elements that include:

- First, self-regulation. As human beings, we self-regulate at our belief level not necessarily our potential level. Our intention is to help you self-regulate much closer to your true potential.

- Second, self-awareness. In order to make the changes, adjustments or modifications needed to achieve your goals, it is first necessary to truly become self-aware of your starting point in relationship to your goal. Our intention is to help you understand what might be blocking you, what you may have locked onto, or possibly the habits, attitudes or beliefs that no longer apply to the person you intend to be.

- Third, motivation. You want the drive, desire, passion that comes with having a clearly defined and accurate purpose. Goals that excite help you put life on a want to, choose to, love to basis rather than coercing or forcing yourself. It is our intention to show you how you can use your mind most effectively to grow yourself into your goals and not throw yourself into them.

- Fourth, empathy. It's about putting yourself in someone else's shoes, being able to see from the other person's perspective. You want to have a good grasp of your own emotions while being considerate of others' emotions. It is our intention that you will understand how your historical memories, negative emotions, and hurtful self-talk are inhibiting the release of your potential and how you might be coaching yourself and those you care about the most backward, away from your goals rather than toward them.

- And finally, adeptness – being highly skilled, proficient, developing an expertise. It is our intention that you not only understand how your mind works, the process of setting and migrating toward you goals, but also it is our intention to compel you to apply that knowledge to your life and toward getting the education and the career that you desire. [Goleman, Boyatzis, McKee (2013) *Primal Leadership: Unleashing the Power of Emotional Intelligence*]

THOUGHT PATTERNS FOR A SUCCESSFUL CAREER®
Mastering the Attitude of Success™ • Participant Manual
©The Pacific Institute®, LLC

2 Context for the Course: HOW?

OVERVIEW

There will be a lot of useful information taught in this course, information that we can apply not only along our path to graduation, but to every part of our life, from here forward. For most of us, it is easiest to learn something new gradually, step by step, applying what we learn as we go. Learning how to think effectively is no different from learning how to add, subtract, multiply and divide – step by step, and applying it as we go forward.

OBJECTIVES

By the end of this unit, I will understand:

- the difference between a fixed mindset and a growth mindset.

- how a growth mindset allows me to release more of my potential.

- that my brain is not carved in stone, but can learn, unlearn and relearn as often as I need it to.

I am smart. I am capable.
Give me the opportunity and I can learn anything.

LouTice

KEY CONCEPTS

Goal(s): A sought end that may be actual and objective, or internal, subjective and operational; conceived future; distal goals are end-results, targets; proximal goals are near-term means to the end-result.

Mindset: A pattern of thought.

Performance: An act or behavior of any kind.

NOTES

Write down your ideas, observations and insights as you work through this unit. Date your entries.

....

....

....

....

....

....

....

....

....

....

....

....

....

....

....

....

....

....

....

REFLECTIVE QUESTIONS

1. This is one instance when I learned something, then needed to unlearn it, in order to re-learn it in a different way:

2. What example do I have, from my own life, where I put forth the effort "above and beyond" and accomplished something?

3. What gave me the willingness to keep working at it until it was accomplished?

THOUGHT PATTERNS FOR A SUCCESSFUL CAREER®
Mastering the Attitude of Success™ • Participant Manual
©The Pacific Institute®, LLC

SUMMARY

HOW are we going to deliver this curriculum?

We are going to lay out scientific research, psychological concepts and timeless principles in step by step, concise segments. Following each segment, you will be presented with application ideas, reflective questions, and exercises so you can put the concepts into practice.

How will you get yourself to practice? We're going to encourage you to have a growth mindset, not a fixed mindset, in order to release your potential.

Dr. Carol Dweck, of Stanford University, describes the fixed mindset as the consuming goal is proving yourself, over and over. You believe your intelligence, personality, and qualities are carved in stone, never to be changed. Every situation calls for you to confirm your personality, character, and intelligence. Every situation is evaluated. Will I succeed or fail? Will I look smart or dumb? Will I be accepted or rejected? Will I feel like a winner or a loser?

On the other hand, this growth mindset is quite the opposite. It is based on the belief that your basic qualities are things that can be developed through your efforts. Effort is the ultimate key and effort doesn't take aptitude or intelligence. It only takes effort. In a fixed mindset, effort is seen as a sign of weakness. If the world sees me as putting forth effort, I must not be smart. I must not be capable. Although each of us is very different in our talents, aptitudes, interests, or personality, everyone can change and grow through application and experience. [Dweck, Carol Ph.D. (2006) *Mindset: The New Psychology of Success*]

How can we be confident that you'll choose a growth mindset? We have science on our side. Dr. Michael Merzenich, often called the Father of Brain Plasticity, explains Plastic Brain Change this way:

- Through our senses of sight, smell, touch, taste, and feel we take in information which is then translated into patterns of electrical impulses that engage the brain. As a skill is developed, the brain creates specific neural pathways until it becomes stronger, faster, more reliable, and more specific to each new task.

- Within our young brain as a baby, toddler, or an adolescent, our plasticity switch is largely left "on" because almost every experience is new. Our brain is a sponge, but as the newness of the information becomes more routine and consistent, the brain resorts to more controlled action. The neural pathways have been developed. So, as our brain matures, it undergoes physical and chemical changes that increase the power of the OFF switch.

- Dr. Merzenich offers a humorous insight: If our brains were constantly changing based on "new" information – in other words if our brain didn't turn off the ON switch – the importance of certain experiences (like sitting) would be highly over-represented in the brain. Since most of us spend a lot of time sitting down, an enormous area in our brains would become dedicated to information from our rear ends, which isn't exactly the best possible use of our brain resources! [Merzenich, Michael Ph.D. (2013) *Soft-Wired: How the New Science of Brain Plasticity Can Change Your Life*]

Here is the most important conclusion for us. Because we have a plastic, not carved in stone brain, we can re-wire, which means learn, unlearn, and re-learn if we choose to turn the switch back ON. How do we do that? By creating circumstances which are largely within our control. First, paying careful attention. Second, focusing on a task or goal. And third, through the positive evaluation of our performance in a goal-directed behavior.

You have enrolled. You have decided that further education is necessary for the job you want, the income you want, the life you want. If that stays within your attention, if it has your focus, and you allow yourself to practice and assimilate the information to come, your brain will be on board.

2

Context for the Course: WHO?

OVERVIEW

Like the ripple effect of a stone being dropped in a pond, this education will ripple out into all areas of life – as individuals, students, and professionals – as well as home, family and leisure. Throughout this course, as we learn the concepts and principles of effective thinking, we will apply them to our goal of graduation, as well as our ultimate goal of living a successful life.

OBJECTIVES

By the end of this unit, I will understand:

- graduation is within my grasp.

- my intent to achieve graduation fuels my energy, drive and creativity to get around any obstacles in my path.

- that by the time I finish this course, I have the soft skills necessary to perform well in my chosen career path.

Everything we do in life ripples out beyond ourselves.
Let's make them positive ripples.

LouTice

KEY CONCEPTS

Create/Creativity: The quality of being creative; the ability to create.

Energy: A force that drives one to a goal.

Goal(s): A sought end that may be actual and objective, or internal, subjective and operational; conceived future; distal goals are end-results, targets; proximal goals are near-term means to the end-result.

NOTES

Write down your ideas, observations and insights as you work through this unit. Date your entries.

....

....

....

....

....

....

....

....

....

....

....

....

....

....

....

....

....

....

....

....

REFLECTIVE QUESTIONS

1. Other than how this applies to completing my education, what other area of my life would I like to focus on while taking this course? (family, relationships, physical health, etc.)

2. What one particular obstacle am I worried will prevent me from completing my education? If it does occur, am I confident that I can invent the "how" to solve it?

3. What do I think are my "top 5" soft skills characteristics that will propel me to get my education and the career I desire?

SUMMARY

WHO will be affected by the outcome of your understanding and applying this education? You, the individual. You, the student. You, the professional.

You the individual: Your relationships, with your family, with those you care about most will be reflected in how you speak to yourself, how you speak to others, and how you apply goal-setting and assimilating in all areas of your life. Your friends and family will see a change in you as you become more confident, self-assured, and deliberate in your thoughts and your actions. When you understand how your mind works, and you deliberately put it into action, you will find yourself causing goals in all areas of your life. As you continue to do so, it begins to snowball and you approach new goals with more excitement, energy, and drive. It's a great cycle to be on.

You the student: You chose to return to school most likely for many reasons, with the idea of a new career, new income, possibly a promotion or more responsibility. But ultimately, it was with the expectation for a better life for both you and your family.

Even through the brief Introduction segments of what is yet to come in the curriculum, you should be convinced that you are most likely fully capable (from an aptitude standpoint). Therefore, if you do not succeed in getting the education you intend, it won't be the hard skills that will let you down, but rather your soft skills. Since you are capable, then you need to focus on making yourself comfortable.

You want to get comfortable with the "new you" that you intend. As the education and process unfolds throughout this curriculum, apply it. Keep the goal of your education solidly in front of you. Keep focused and pay careful attention to where you are going. Unfortunately, life happens. Adversity and obstacles will show themselves along the way. Just know that the creativity, effort, energy, drive, and problem-solving to overcome, get around or go through, will come. It won't be because you need to know "how" you are going to get past those obstacles at this very moment. By keeping the goal of an education in front of you, you will create the how.

And finally, you the professional: The soft skill abilities that will drive you toward your education are also the characteristics that employers want most when hiring. Consider the following Top Five Characteristics:

- O*NET (U.S. clearinghouse of occupational information) [http://www.onetcenter.org]
    - Critical Thinking
    - Complex Problem Solving
    - Judgment and Decision-Making
    - Active Listening
    - Computers and Electronics

- From Research organizations like National Association of Colleges and Employers [https://www.naceweb.org]
    - Ability to work in a team
    - Ability to make decisions and solve problems
    - Ability to plan, organize and prioritize work
    - Ability to communicate verbally with people inside and outside an organization
    - Ability to obtain and process information

- From job sites like Glassdoor [http://www.glassdoor.com/blog/8-traits-employers/]
  - Comfortable confidence
  - Willingness to listen and learn
  - Adaptability
  - Flexibility
  - Self-reliance

- Career Attraction [http://www.careerattraction.com/become-the-perfect-job-applicant-15-traits-employers-look-for-when-hiring/]
  - Leadership-oriented
  - Resilient
  - Candid
  - Competitive
  - In-control

- From Magazines like Forbes® [http://www.forbes.com/sites/meghancasserly/2012/10/04/top-five-personality-traits-employers-hire-most/]
  - Professionalism
  - High-energy
  - Confidence
  - Self-monitoring
  - Intellectual curiosity

- And US News and World Report [http://money.usnews.com/money/blogs/outside-voices-careers/2013/09/10/5-employee-qualities-on-every-employers-wish-list]
  - Empathy
  - Mentoring
  - Interpersonal Skills
  - Self-direction and initiative
  - Flex and adaptability

The skill sets most wanted by employers are also the skill sets that will get you through your education in the first place. Daniel Robbins reports that companies are now looking at the emotional aspect of intelligence of applicants and employees in deciding whom to hire or whom to keep and whom to let go. According to studies, EQ predicts higher performance three times better than IQ.

If you are not convinced yet, it's not just in hiring. Daniel Goleman, Richard Boyatzis and Annie McKee found that when star performers were matched against average ones in senior leadership positions, about 85% of the difference in their profiles was attributable to emotional intelligence factors rather than to purely cognitive abilities like technical expertise.

TO SUM IT ALL UP....

The technical, analytical skills that you will receive through your academic institution will satisfy the price of entry into your field of study. However, it does not make an employee superior in terms of performance. It is the understanding and application of your soft skill, emotional intelligence abilities that will propel you, not only through your education, but also your career.

The application of the curriculum and process unfolded for you depends mostly on your soft skills, not your hard skills. It is our intention that through the understanding and repeated practice of the principles, in the segments to follow, that you will grow as an individual, as a student, and as a professional.

SO, ARE YOU READY TO GO?

NOTES

3 Out of Order / Into Order
Creating and Resolving Discontent with Our Goals

OVERVIEW

When we have a goal, either one we set or is set for us, discontent is created in our human system. As humans, we need to make the picture we hold in our minds match the outside picture. If the internal picture is stronger, we make the outside change and we can stay the same. When the outside picture – the new picture created by the new goal – is stronger, we change our internal picture and grow into the new.

OBJECTIVES

By the end of this unit, I will understand:

- in order to grow and change, I need to create my own discontent with the present.

- I move toward the strongest picture I hold in my mind.

- I am in charge of creating my future.

There is no growth without discontent.

LouTice

KEY CONCEPTS

Dominant Idea: The prevailing view; the strongest picture; a ruling view or belief that is primary.

Gestalt: Human beings are always working to complete the incomplete, working for closure; discrepancy production, discrepancy reduction; a view that psychological phenomena could only be understood if viewed as organized, structured wholes (Gestalten). The Gestalt point of view challenged the idea that phenomena could be introspectively broken down into primitive perceptual elements, for such analysis left out the notion of the whole unitary essence of the phenomena.

Goal(s): A sought end that may be actual and objective, or internal, subjective and operational; conceived future; distal goals are end-results, targets; proximal goals are near-term means to the end-result.

Goal-Setting: The act of establishing what we want.

NOTES

Write down your ideas, observations and insights as you work through this unit. Date your entries.

....

....

....

....

....

....

....

....

....

....

....

....

....

....

....

....

....

....

....

....

REFLECTIVE QUESTIONS

1. What goals do I have that are not causing me some discontent?

   My goals are causing me some discontent because it is requiring me to look for new employment after over 25 years with the same company. I feel I do not have the self discipline or self confidence to believe I can find a new job that will provide the financial stability I need / my family needs.

2. Is this because the picture of the new goal is not strong enough, or that I already know how to accomplish the goal?

   I do not have a solution for my situation but being that I have committed to completing my education, I will write down my goals and review them daily.

3. What can I do to make the picture of the new goal stronger, causing significant discontent within me, and drive myself to what I want?

   I will write down my goals and a plan of action. I will start every day with a job search. I will go to the job placement office at Empire until I am able to find employment

EXERCISE: Out of Order – What Am I Missing?

Joe Pace / Lou Tice

We know that our minds desire order. So, either the internal picture changes, or the external picture changes. Sometimes our minds build obstacles to seeing all that is around us. For this exercise, explore any obstacles you may have with each situation. Have you observed other people create solutions to the same challenge? What is the best solution for you, right now?

SITUATION	What am I not seeing?	What solutions have I seen others come up with?	What is the best short-term solution for me while in school?
Lack of Finances	Have someone else evaluate my finances + budget	– Receive financial aid – parents – Refinance home	student loans until I refinance or use HELOC
Lack of Family Support	N/A I have family support ☺	—	—
Lack of Time	Create a schedule for homework requirement	create schedule	create schedule
Challenges with Technology	possible youtube tutorials	Use additional lab time	ask kids for help
Child Care Issues	N/A	—	—
Health Issues	N/A	—	—
Transportation Issues	N/A	—	—

SUMMARY: Application — Out of Order

Does part, or possibly most, of your decision to enroll in higher education have a lot to do with:

- Wanting new job?

- Wanting a promotion in a current job and more responsibility?

- Wanting a better income?

- Wanting a better life or better opportunities for your children?

- Or simply just wanting an education or skill or trade or certification vs. not having one?

With the very act of enrolling into higher education, you caused a problem for yourself. You decided that you are no longer content with your current job, current income, current level of responsibility, current living situation or current level of education. Instead, you desire to make a change. You want the new opportunities that this education, skill or trade is going to provide for you.

Close your eyes for a moment. What would it look like, feel like, be like as a graduate? What does it look like when you are using your newly acquired skill sets in a new career or at a new level of responsibility? What might your new living situation look like? What new resources and opportunities are you able to provide for your family, or those close to you, because you have completed your training?

Your task is to identify, clarify and repeat that image to yourself over and over so it drives you to complete the task of getting your education. The more vivid the image, the more you are drawn toward it. The more vivid the image, the more you use your mind, deliberately and intentionally, to make it happen and the less you get caught up in the distractions along the way. You realize the parts are pieces of the whole, but not greater than the whole.

THOUGHT PATTERNS FOR A SUCCESSFUL CAREER®
Mastering the Attitude of Success™ • Participant Manual
©The Pacific Institute®, LLC

SUMMARY – APPLICATION: Making the Pictures Match

Joining an exercise facility, or enrolling in school, and being successful, are very much the same to our brain. From the moment we enroll and attend our first class, or the first time we show up at the gym, our mind has the job of keeping us in or getting us out. Our mind is asking, "Is this the new expectation?" "Is this the new me?" "Is this going to be the dominant picture?" "Should I begin acquiring new habits, attitudes, and beliefs to support this new goal?"

We begin to use our energy, motivation, problem-solving and creativity to gather information. We look for resources, support, and evidence to match the strongest picture inside of us. The question becomes, is the strongest picture to stay in or get out? Just because we set the goal doesn't mean our brain will get on board to make it happen. It is through the process of assimilating that goal that our brain shifts into gear to achieve our new goal.

Every time you think about going to the gym or you actually do go, do you find more reasons why you love it? Do you realize how good you feel? Can you tell how much energy you have? Or do you find the opposite? When obstacles occur while you are going to school – child care, transportation, finances, illnesses, or family situations – do you see resources, opportunities, services, and solutions that allow you to overcome the challenges? Or do see the opposite?

There is great power in embracing the strongest picture of you as a graduate and what it can do for you. What percentage of dropouts, from your academic institution, do you think made the decision to leave school because of these reasons?

- lack of finances

- lack of family support

- lack of time

- challenges with technology

- child care issues

- health issues

- transportation issues

This list of seven obstacles probably covers 80% to 90% of the reasons why those students decided that they had drop out. They gave up and couldn't continue.

Let's think about the graduates. What percentage of those graduates from your academic institution had those same obstacles along the way to graduation? Experience tells us the answer is "most," and yet they graduated.

What was the difference between the student who persisted and the student who dropped out? How were some able see solutions and stay in school whereas the others couldn't? How did some find the drive, energy, problem-solving and creativity to find more time in their days? How did some scrape together a few dollars during tough times? How many walked, rode a bike or hitched a ride when necessary? And how many managed to find their cousin's girlfriend's sister, who happened to know a lady, who has a brother who dates a girl, who happens to be a wonderful person, loves children and would love to watch their children while they went to school?

The more dominant the picture in your mind of what you expect, the bigger the problem you give your brain. You brain needs to work to solve it. It wants to make the outside picture match the picture you hold in your mind. Give your brain a chance to take you through to the completion of your education by assimilating your graduation – starting today.

THOUGHT PATTERNS FOR A SUCCESSFUL CAREER®
Mastering the Attitude of Success™ • Participant Manual
©The Pacific Institute®, LLC

SECTION 2: CORE COMPETENCIES

This Section contains the Core Algorithm of The Pacific Institute's curriculum.

- TPSC MAS Inventory Pre-Assessment

- Course Overview: I Am Ready for This!

- Unit 1: What Else Am I Leaving Out?

- Unit 2: How My Mind Works

- Unit 3: From My Toolbox: The Reticular Activating System

- Unit 4: The "Truth" is What We Believe It Is

- Unit 5: My Internal Conversation – 24/7/365

- Unit 6: What Can I Make Happen for Me?

- Unit 7: My Habits and Attitudes

- Unit 8: Comfort Zones

- Unit 9: Setting Benchmarks for My Future

- Unit 10: From My Toolbox: Change Made Easy

- Unit 11: Seeing Myself in the Future

- Unit 12: It's My Choice

The TPSC MAS Pre-and Post-Inventory is designed as a self-assessment to take before beginning, and after completing, this curriculum.

Read each statement carefully. Circle the response that best fits your judgement at the moment:

- SA = Strongly Agree

- A = Agree

- MA = Mildly Agree

- MD = Mildly Disagree

- D = Disagree

- SD = Strong Disagree

There are no right or wrong answers to the assessment. This is simply your perceptions of the questions being asked.

You are encouraged to take the pre-assessment before beginning Section 2, the Core of the curriculum. This provides you with a baseline from which to measure your growth. When you have completed this course, take the post-assessment, found at the end of Section 3 – the Extended Learning units.

By taking the five to eight minutes to complete the assessment, you have the opportunity to self-assess your perceptions of what you have learned from the concepts in this curriculum.

TPSC MAS Inventory Pre-Assessment

Please read each statement and circle the response that most accurately describes your beliefs and/or feelings.

		Strongly Agree	Agree	Mildly Agree	Mildly Disagree	Disagree	Strongly Disagree
1.	When I enter a new situation, I typically see others as smarter than me.	SA	A	MA	MD	D	SD
2.	My past successes are due to luck.	SA	A	MA	MD	D	SD
3.	In order to achieve a goal, I need to know how I intend to make it happen when I start.	SA	A	MA	MD	D	SD
4.	When I get a good grade it is because I caused it.	SA	A	MA	MD	D	SD
5.	I have complete control of my attitude.	SA	A	MA	MD	D	SD
6.	I am accountable for the goals I set.	SA	A	MA	MD	D	SD
7.	Outside events have a great impact on my life.	SA	A	MA	MD	D	SD
8.	When I am "stuck in my ways," there is no changing me.	SA	A	MA	MD	D	SD
9.	My past successes are because of me.	SA	A	MA	MD	D	SD
10.	When I achieve a goal, it is because I was fortunate.	SA	A	MA	MD	D	SD
11.	I know how my self-talk impacts my attitude.	SA	A	MA	MD	D	SD
12.	I am responsible for my own beliefs.	SA	A	MA	MD	D	SD
13.	My happiness is increased when my goals are met.	SA	A	MA	MD	D	SD
14.	Goal setting is a waste of time.	SA	A	MA	MD	D	SD
15.	It is next to impossible for me to change habits that I have had over most of my lifetime.	SA	A	MA	MD	D	SD
16.	I know how to set goals.	SA	A	MA	MD	D	SD
17.	When I do the work, I can do well on most any assignment.	SA	A	MA	MD	D	SD
18.	I can "turn off" my self talk when it's negative.	SA	A	MA	MD	D	SD
19.	I know how to control my own self-talk	SA	A	MA	MD	D	SD
20.	Good things happen to me because I cause them.	SA	A	MA	MD	D	SD
21.	I have limited control over making changes in me.	SA	A	MA	MD	D	SD
22.	When I set my goals, I get a vivid picture of what I intend.	SA	A	MA	MD	D	SD
23.	I typically need others to solve my problems.	SA	A	MA	MD	D	SD
24.	Despite the attitudes of others around me, I decide my own attitude.	SA	A	MA	MD	D	SD
25.	I know how my self-talk impacts my feelings.	SA	A	MA	MD	D	SD
26.	I let negative past experiences influence my current decisions.	SA	A	MA	MD	D	SD
27.	I know the feeling of wanting something so badly that I can "taste" it.	SA	A	MA	MD	D	SD
28.	It is my choice to be whatever I want to be in life.	SA	A	MA	MD	D	SD
29.	I know how to set goals so that they will become reality.	SA	A	MA	MD	D	SD
30.	When I believe I can do something, I do it.	SA	A	MA	MD	D	SD
31.	If I get a poor grade on a test, it is mostly because of factors outside of my control.	SA	A	MA	MD	D	SD

32.	I let negative opinions from others affect me.	SA	A	MA	MD	D	SD
33.	When I fail to achieve a goal, it is my own fault.	SA	A	MA	MD	D	SD
34.	My negative self-talk leads to negative actions toward others.	SA	A	MA	MD	D	SD
35	I am accountable for my own actions regardless of the situation.	SA	A	MA	MD	D	SD
36.	I typically picture what I want before I get it.	SA	A	MA	MD	D	SD
37.	When I set my mind to it, I make things happen.	SA	A	MA	MD	D	SD
38.	When I don't get support from others, I often give up on my goals.	SA	A	MA	MD	D	SD
39.	Changing a habit is up to me.	SA	A	MA	MD	D	SD
40.	I give up on my goals at some point, because I realize I am not capable.	SA	A	MA	MD	D	SD
41.	Due to past negative experiences, I don't have high expectations of doing well in my courses.	SA	A	MA	MD	D	SD
42.	Writing down my goals is a regular event for me.	SA	A	MA	MD	D	SD
43.	My current study habits are good enough to cause the grades I expect.	SA	A	MA	MD	D	SD
44.	I often picture or imagine what it will look like when I achieve my goals.	SA	A	MA	MD	D	SD
45.	Attending or Logging into my class is an important daily routine.	SA	A	MA	MD	D	SD
46.	I often think about what it will feel like when I accomplish my goals.	SA	A	MA	MD	D	SD
47.	Becoming comfortable in a new situation is within my control.	SA	A	MA	MD	D	SD
48.	When I make up my mind, I cannot be deterred.	SA	A	MA	MD	D	SD
49.	When a task is difficult for me, I tend to quit.	SA	A	MA	MD	D	SD
50.	When I feel out of place, I look to get out as fast as I can.	SA	A	MA	MD	D	SD
51.	When I want something, I make it happen.	SA	A	MA	MD	D	SD
52.	My attitude and the achievement of my goals are not related.	SA	A	MA	MD	D	SD
53.	It is not possible to change a belief.	SA	A	MA	MD	D	SD
54.	I am quick to find excuses when I give up on a goal.	SA	A	MA	MD	D	SD
55.	Most of my current responsibilities are things I choose to do.	SA	A	MA	MD	D	SD
56.	I review my goals on a daily basis.	SA	A	MA	MD	D	SD
57.	When I succeed, it is mostly because of me.	SA	A	MA	MD	D	SD
58.	I have accepted others' opinions of me as truth; they are currently holding me back.	SA	A	MA	MD	D	SD
59.	When I fail, it is typically due to factors outside of my control.	SA	A	MA	MD	D	SD
60.	I have experienced the feeling of having a goal become a part of me.	SA	A	MA	MD	D	SD

Assessment developed by Dr. Scott Fitzgibbon and Dr. Joe Pace

I Am Ready for This!
From Good Ideas to Great Achievement

COURSE OVERVIEW

In the past, we were happy with just having had ideas. Some were good, some were not, and some we managed to realize. However, there wasn't any consistency in realizing some of our ideas. As we move through this course, we will discover a way to consistently take our ideas and turn them into realities – we will turn them into goals.

COURSE OBJECTIVES

By the end of this unit, I will understand:

- that it isn't enough to just have good ideas.

- I need to take my best ideas and turn them into goals.

- the process for turning my ideas into achievable goals.

In order to move forward, having an idea is not good enough.
We need to have very clear goals.

LouTice

KEY CONCEPTS

Assimilate/Assimilation: The incorporating of an idea or thought into the subconscious; the absorption or process of incorporating something external into one's cognitive processes; making new visions a part of our lives; e.g., one learns and can behaviorally manifest mastery of fundamental mathematical processes.

Goal(s): A sought end that may be actual and objective, or internal, subjective and operational; conceived future; distal goals are end-results, targets; proximal goals are near-term means to the end-result.

Goal-Setting: The act of establishing what we want.

Ideas: A product of thought.

THOUGHT PATTERNS FOR A SUCCESSFUL CAREER®
Mastering the Attitude of Success™ • Participant Manual
©The Pacific Institute®, LLC

NOTES

Write down your ideas, observations and insights as you work through this unit. Date your entries.

REFLECTIVE QUESTIONS

1. To me, what is the difference between having an idea and having a goal?

2. With completing my education as my goal, what are some specific actions I intend to take?

3. Based on my experience with my education in the past, what do I intend to do differently this time?

4. If, in the future, I begin to contemplate quitting, what will I say to me to get me back on track?

EXERCISE: Record Your Own Evidence

• When in your life, whether you were 6, 12, or 18 did you want something so badly that it was all you could focus on? Describe it fully below.

• Did you get it or at least come close? Describe the outcome below.

• Was the picture in your mind so vivid that you didn't give yourself the option to fail? What did it look like?

• Did you have to block the negativity of others around you who tried to take your goal away from you? How did you shut out others' comments?

• Did your self-talk continually take you toward your goal or away from it?

EXERCISE: Moving My Ideas into My Goals

For this exercise, list some great ideas you have had in the past year in the left column. In the middle, identify which of these great ideas you want to move into goals. In the right column, jot down some tactics you can use, in order to begin to move your ideas into goals.

RECENT "GREAT IDEAS"	IDEAS I INTEND TO MOVE INTO GOALS	HOW I WILL BEGIN

THOUGHT PATTERNS FOR A SUCCESSFUL CAREER®
Mastering the Attitude of Success™ • Participant Manual
©The Pacific Institute®, LLC

SUMMARY: Fundamentals =Video

When a goal stays in the forefront of our minds, because it is aligned with our values and our purpose, the motivation to navigate obstacles, overcome challenges, and power through barriers happens as a direct result of our intentions. With deliberate focus and attention on what we expect, we set up our brain, and thus ourselves, for success.

Having the idea first is vital to the process. It is the genesis of a goal. But what is the difference between having an idea and having a goal?

That question should generate a lot of thought. We need to be specific and accurate about what we intend. We need a plan. We need to commit. We need to hold ourselves accountable. We need to have an end time. But ultimately, the bottom-line difference is, we need to do something. When it was just an idea, there was no obligation to do anything. The biggest difference between an idea and a goal is "action." We are no longer content with the dream, the idea of being or having or doing. Instead, we intend to make it happen.

That's a big jump. For many of us, the idea of enrolling in higher education may have been an idea – a great idea – for a long time. Maybe it wasn't just our idea. As we all know, we have lots of people in our world who are more than willing to share their ideas with us as to what we should do, or how we should live our lives. We probably have many friends and family members whose best ideas seem to be for other people. And when they share those ideas with us about what we should do with our lives, it's very satisfying for them. They get that look in the eye like, "Job well done! I'm good at this. Now that I'm done with you, I'm going to find someone else and tell them how to fix their life, too." It's not hard to have ideas and it's really not hard to have ideas for other people.

It is a big step to make that idea a goal and even a bigger step to make that goal a part of us. This is the process of going from Goal-Setting to Goal-Assimilating. When we assimilate, we absorb. We take it in and make it a part of us.

Let's go back to the idea of enrolling in higher education. If you are participating in this course, you have made the important step of goal-setting. It's no longer just an idea. You have put your thought into action. But in order to complete your education, to graduate, you need to take the next step of Goal-Setting to Goal-Assimilating. It's in this intentional process that all the marvels of the brain, through deliberate attention and focus on our goals and through the continual evaluation of all that you are doing to cause your goal, that our brain releases its wonderful potential. It's not magic. It's being intentional and deliberate. It's taking control of what it is that we expect in life.

It is this process that we will unfold for you in the following units. We will lay out scientific research, psychological concepts, and timeless principles in step-by-step, concise segments. We will use discussion, reflection, and exercises to enhance understanding, and encourage all to apply it – which means practice, practice, practice, repeat, repeat, repeat. All those ideas we have had and most specifically this one – getting our education – isn't as far off as we think, if we are willing to apply the best of what we know as to how our brain works for us.

NOTES

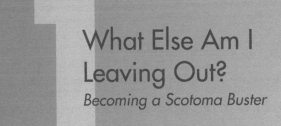

What Else Am I Leaving Out?
Becoming a Scotoma Buster

OVERVIEW

The question we must all ask ourselves is, "Am I seeing all there is to see?" Most of us don't realize that we don't see everything because of the *way* we were raised, *where* we were raised and *how* we were taught. We spent our lives listening to others tell us "the way it is," and we believed them. The good news is that we *can see* more than we have seen in the past, and this will open up a new future for us in our education, and our lives.

OBJECTIVES

By the end of this unit, I will understand:

- scotomas and how they can limit me in school, at home, and in all parts of my life.

- by locking on to the way things have always been done, I am blind to new possibilities.

- I need to be mindful of the "truths" that are given to me, even from teachers and loved ones, as they may not be my truths.

*When my mind is fixed, I do not allow myself
to live the life I am capable of living.*

LouTice

KEY CONCEPTS

Conditioning: a predisposition to a mode of behavior given the appropriate stimulus.

Potential: having the strong possibility for development into a state of actuality; latent.

Scotoma: Greek for "blind spot" or blindness; blind spots in our awareness as a result of preconceived ideas and conditioning. For example, if we believe that everything about a person or situation is bad, it will be difficult or impossible for us to see the good.

NOTES

Write down your ideas, observations and insights as you work through this unit. Date your entries.

REFLECTIVE QUESTIONS

1. Up until today, who has helped me make up my mind about my education and career possibilities?

2. Do I believe that I am worthy of higher education? Why?

3. Here is why I believe I am capable of achieving both the education and the career I want:

EXERCISE: 9 Dots

Connect the nine dots using ONLY four straight lines, WITHOUT lifting your pen.

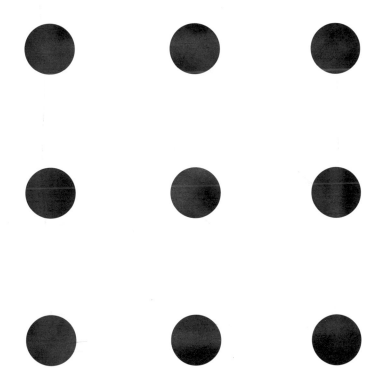

EXERCISE: Maze

The objective is to get from gate A to gate B, without crossing any lines, in the quickest time.

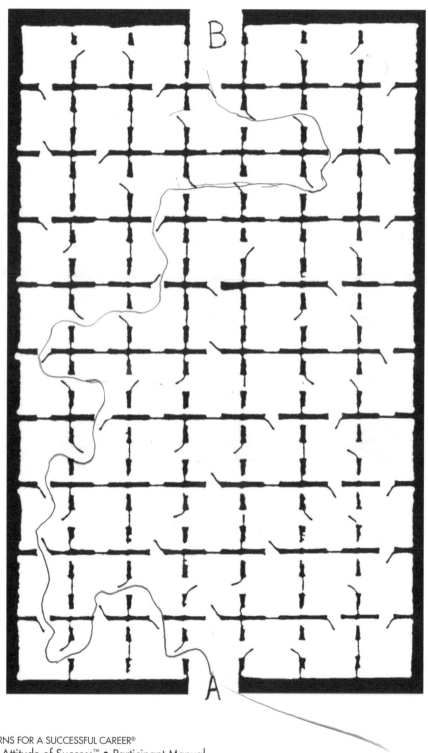

EXERCISE: Do You Have a Scotoma?

SAND *(box drawing)* 1 *sand box*	MAN *over* BOARD 2	STAND I *under* 3	R|E|A|D|I|N|G *reading between* 4 *the lines*
WEAR LONG *long "under" wear* 5	R ROAD A D 6 *cross road*	T O W N V = ↓ ⑦ *down town*	CYCLE CYCLE CYCLE *tricycle* 8
LE VEL *split level* 9	0 / M.D. B.A. PH.D. 10 *3 degrees below*	KNEE LIGHT *Knee "on" light* 11	ii OO OO OO OO *Circles under eyes.* ⑫
[HAIR 13 *high chair*	*(two dice) 6 7* ⑭	T O U C H *touch down* V ↓ 15	GROUND *(feet)* 16 *6 ft under ground*
over MIND MATTER 17	HE'S/HIMSELF *beside* 18	ECNALG *backwards glance* 19	DEATH LIFE *life after death.* 20

EXERCISE: Be Careful What We Lock On To

"What is it?"

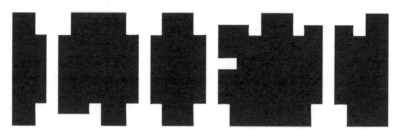

"What is it?"

EXERCISE: Be Careful What We Lock On To

Bunny/Duck

"What is it?"

Please count the number of triangles in the diagram. Count carefully! After you have carefully counted the triangles, answer the questions on the following page.

EXERCISE: Be Careful What We Lock On To

1. Because of the instruction under the diagram, did you happen to lock on to the idea that there were actually triangles there?

   Yes.

2. When thinking about your upcoming courses, what truths about yourself have you locked onto? (For example: I have always been good at math, but please don't make me give a presentation in front of others!)

   I enjoy math but sometimes make very dumb mistakes because I go too fast.

3. Who convinced you of this? Is it possible that they (and you) are wrong about your potential?

   I convinced myself.

EXERCISE: Opinions, Beliefs and the Truth

For each of your current beliefs in column 1, fill in what others have said to you in column 2, and then whether those opinions have shaped your belief in a positive or negative manner.

1	2	3
What are some of my current beliefs with regard to…	What are some of the opinions that others have shared with me regarding their view of my potential?	How have the opinions of others shaped my belief: Positively or Negatively?
Completing my Education	I have been told by many people that I can complete my education	This has encouraged me to finally do it.
Starting the career I want	My friends and family have motivated me to transition in my career.	This too has been a positive influence
Getting the salary I want	I am very lucky that I already have a good salary	I want to prove to myself that I can get that salary anywhere *not only where I am.*
Setting Goals		
Creating the future I want		

SUMMARY: Fundamentals

Now, since you are taking this course through a school, we started you off with a test. It wasn't difficult, but what we learned was fascinating. First we got locked on to Roman numerals, which are different from what we use every day, so that pattern affected our perception. Then, because most of the Roman numerals involve bold, straight lines, we locked on to straight lines. So, when it came time to come up with the solution, we were locked into a perception "box" that favored straight lines.

How often have we created our own perception boxes, based upon what we hear or see? And how have those limited perceptions helped make up our minds about how we would think in the future?

Ever since we were little, we have been absorbing – like huge sponges – everything that has gone on around us. Everything! Now because some things we didn't understand, like foreign languages, we learned to ignore them. Because something over here caught our eyes, we didn't see what was going on over there. This is natural, because our minds can really only concentrate on one thing at a time – despite what the "multi-taskers" say.

When we block information coming in from our senses, we build what is called a "scotoma." S-C-O-T-O-M-A. "Scotoma" is Greek for blindness or blind spot. We can build scotomas to information coming from all of our senses. When we concentrate while reading, we block out sounds and smells. Are you wearing a watch or a ring? Did you feel it before I asked about it? Probably not.

The problem with scotomas is that we don't know we have them. We always think we are seeing the truth. In fact, our minds conspire to help us believe we are seeing the truth, even when our minds know better.

For example, have you ever lost the keys to your car or home. You are running around your house or apartment, searching for the keys you have told yourself you lost. Then, a friend or relative stops you, points to the table right in front of you, and says, "There they are." And what is your first reaction? "Who moved them?!? They weren't there a minute ago!" Of course, they were there. They've been there all along. Because you told yourself you had "lost" your keys, your mind made sure you wouldn't see them. It built a scotoma for you! You locked on to "I lost my keys," so your mind locked the keys out of your visual field.

While we all have scotomas, they aren't always easy to find. If you find yourself working hard and not getting the results you want, look for a scotoma. Ask people you trust to help you by asking, "What am I not seeing?" Sometimes, looking at a problem from a different angle will help us find the scotomas.

As you build your future, and build your life, if you don't know about scotomas, you give up quickly. You take the wrong solution. You think, "I can't get it through my thick head. "Everybody else seems to get it. I just don't get it. I must be stupid." Now, you don't want to do that, because then you start acting like you're stupid.

There's a principle I want you to remember: We behave and act, not in accordance with the truth, but the truth as we believe it to be. When we lock on to a belief, it won't let us see people, business opportunities, answers or solutions. Honest to goodness, our beliefs just don't let us see all there is to see.

Most people don't know they have scotomas. When you're stuck and you can't see the answers – to building your business, creating your future or you can't see the answer and can't hear what somebody is saying – don't give up. You are probably just full of scotomas.

Whenever I'm stuck and I want to build my business or I want to grow and don't know how, I don't care if I don't know how. I'll find the way. I persist, because I know the answers exist. Somebody sees them, even if I don't.

The most important thing to know is that you are so smart. You are so capable. You can build your future. You don't even need to know where the answers are coming from. I just want to encourage you that, as you approach your careers and school, don't be intimidated by them!

For the best results, start with the premise that the answer exists, we just don't see it yet.

SUMMARY: Application

It was the 5th grade. After being out of school for several days with some kind of illness I returned. On my first day back, Miss Z asked everyone in class to line up in front of the room. We were going to participate in a spelling bee. Now, historical memory up to that point in 5th grade was that I had always been a good speller. I had always done well in spelling bees, being one of the last couple of kids left standing. I was definitely never the first to sit or get teased by the other kids because I misspelled a word.

However, on this occasion, I hadn't even seen the words in the unit because I had been out of school. But rather than being intimidated or worrying about the fact that I hadn't seen the words, I was confident. I was actually looking forward to the challenge of spelling words from a list that I hadn't even seen. I was full of high self-efficacy or high causative power. I knew I was going to shine.

Miss Z starts working her way through the first couple of kids, giving them words, which I am spelling in my own mind. I'm feeling even more confident since I knew how to spell every word. Then she comes to me. She looks up from the list and says, "Your word is OREO." Instantly, my heart started beating through my chest. My face turned red. My mouth dried, and my mind went blank – well, mostly blank.

Now, I am 11 years old, and completely flabbergasted. So, rather than ask Miss Z for a definition, or possibly asking her to use the word in a sentence, I was consumed with only one thought: How is the cookie in our spelling book?

After what seemed to be an eternity of everyone staring at me, I spelled the only OREO in my world: O-R-E-O. As soon as the last O left my mouth, the entire class, including Miss Z, erupted in laughter. Completely embarrassed and frankly confused, I headed for my seat, the first to sit.

Paul Brainard, the next kid in line, spelled the bird, ORIOLE. As it turns out, Miss Z was not from western Pennsylvania, so as I and most others from western Pennsylvania would have pronounced the word "oriole" (emphasizing the L), she pronounced it "oreo." I somehow got the label "cookie boy" from my classmates who persisted with the teasing.

The next day in health class, Miss Z had decided (while I was out sick I'm sure – conspiracy theory) that we were going to pronounce and spell our health words. Each child would pronounce the word, then look up from the book, and spell the word out loud. Fresh off the devastating experience from the day before, I was already feeling panicky over what my word was going to be, and if I was going to be able to pronounce and spell it in front of my classmates. So as we started going around the room, I was completely oblivious to anything the other kids were doing. The only thing I could focus on was counting the kids, counting the words, counting the kids and counting the words, until I came to my word. I looked at my word and if I could have given up school for the rest of my life at that moment in order to get out of there, I would have. Not only couldn't I spell, but now I can't even pronounce the word in front of me!

I looked at the word for what seemed an eternity and finally looked up. Again, everyone was staring at me. And in front of those same 11 year olds who had been teasing me since the day before, I pronounced, "es o PHA' gus." Once again, I brought down the house, the laughter from the other kids deafening. This is your "e SOPH' a gus." It is my "es o PHA' gus."

My spelling and health grades took a dive. It wasn't that I didn't have the potential. I had always gotten good grades in both prior to that fatal week. But it all got locked under negative, embarrassing, and debilitating emotions. Future decisions with regard to my ability to do well in either subject were heavily affected by that horrible week.

Where might you have locked onto a similar fate? Where have you locked onto, built a huge scotoma to, your actual ability in certain subjects or course content? Now that ability is locked under negative experiences from the past. You can change it if you choose to, and that's what this curriculum and process is all about.

How My Mind Works
Uncovering the Power in the Thought Process

OVERVIEW

As scientists unravel the mysteries of the human brain – the magnificent complexity of its structure – we have discovered the levels of the mind involved in the thought process. Our conscious, subconscious and creative subconscious levels work together to perceive the world around us, store our reality and make sure that each of us acts like the person we know ourselves to be.

OBJECTIVES

By the end of this unit, I will understand:

- the four parts of the decision-making process: Perception, Association, Evaluation, and finally, making Decisions.

- that all of my history is stored in my Subconscious, everything that has happened around me, and includes how I felt about each event.

- how each level of my mind works together to keep me "like me" – but the "me" of my past.

When we speak about the mind,
we are talking about the brain in action.

LouTice

KEY CONCEPTS

Conscious: the aspect of mind that encompasses all that one is currently are of; that is, those aspects of mental life that one is attending to.

Subconscious: the level of mind through which material passes on the way toward full consciousness; an information store containing memories that are momentarily outside of awareness but that can be easily brought into consciousness.

Creative Subconscious: the source of mental processes that lead to solutions, ideas, conceptualizations, artistic forms, theories or products that are unique and novel. Self-regulating mechanism for behavior.

NOTES

Write down your ideas, observations and insights as you work through this unit. Date your entries.

....

....

....

....

....

....

....

....

....

....

....

....

....

....

....

....

....

....

....

REFLECTIVE QUESTIONS

1. What are some "educational realities" of my past that could affect my decision-making about courses or subjects in my future?

2. When and where did some of these experiences happen?

3. Are these experiences, and the emotions I attached to them, still valid as I move forward with my education and career?

EXERCISE: Meaningful Change

We constantly compare current perceptions against our historical memory. If something similar happened to us in the past, it is a meaningful memory. If we compare and there is nothing in our memory, it is meaningless in helping us deal with the current situation. Select from the list below two experiences that are meaningful to you. Then, run them through the Thought Process to see how the past might be influencing your present decisions.

- Dropping out of school

- Struggling to understand course content

- Partying rather than studying for an exam

- Presenting in front of an audience

- Taking a mid-term or final exam

- Deciding whether or not to go to school today

- Procrastinating, filling my time with "busy work" and avoiding what needs to be done

PERCEPTION	ASSOCIATION	EVALUATION	DECISION	CONCLUSION
New information through my senses	Have I seen this before?	What is this probably leading me to?	Based on what can be or has been	Do I want to fix it or not?
Example: New relationship possibility	Yes, a couple of serious ones	Ended in heartache and lost friends	Choose not to get involved with new person because of past	If I want new relationship, I need to not let past negative feelings affect my current decision

EXERCISE: Maintaining Sanity

In the table below, we track how our perceptions of our abilities affect our decisions. Study the example below, then move to the next page and work through the exercise with some perceptions of your own abilities, what has caused them, and what you want to do to fix it and move forward.

Example:

MY PERCEPTION	HOW DID I GET THE NEGATIVE HISTORICAL MEMORY?	WHAT DOES MY CREATIVE SUBCONSCIOUS DO TO MAINTAIN SANITY?	WHAT AM I GOING TO DO TO FIX IT?
Not good in Math	• algebra class in high school. Did not understand what teacher was saying • got yelled at when I asked questions • teacher threw chalk at the walls when I still didn't get it • was humiliated in front of my classmates at the chalkboard	• gives me a "million" reasons to skip class • mind constantly wanders when I do go to class • always seem to be tired because the teacher is boring • never have enough time to do homework.	• discover other students in class who are "afraid" also • promise to look after each other since we have the same fears • make a vow to never miss class • find a classmate who is willing to be an accountability partner • Make sure that homework is always done first • see a tutor immediately if I don't understand something

THOUGHT PATTERNS FOR A SUCCESSFUL CAREER®
Mastering the Attitude of Success™ • Participant Manual
©The Pacific Institute®, LLC

EXERCISE: Maintaining Sanity, Part 2

Work through the exercise with a couple perceptions of your own abilities. List what has caused them, how your Subconscious keeps you sane, and what you want to do to fix it and move forward. (Use this same method to address other perceptions of your abilities.)

MY PERCEPTION	HOW DID I GET THE NEGATIVE HISTORICAL MEMORY?	WHAT DOES MY CREATIVE SUBCONSCIOUS DO TO MAINTAIN SANITY?	WHAT AM I GOING TO DO TO FIX IT?

SUMMARY: Fundamentals

First, let's get one thing straight: when we talk about "the mind" we are talking about the brain in action. It's a little like your car – you know the engine and drive train are making you move, but you don't see every little piece actually doing the work! Your mind is moving you along, but you don't actually see the neurons firing in the different parts of your brain.

In order for us to make sense of how your mind works, we break it into three parts: the Conscious, the Subconscious, and the Creative Subconscious. It's a bit like an iceberg. What appears above the surface of the ocean is like your Conscious Mind, and it is only a small part of the total iceberg. Your Subconscious and Creative Subconscious sit below the surface, reacting like an iceberg to the currents and water temperature, only they are reacting to what you are perceiving from the world around you.

The problem with most of us is we don't respect our subconscious enough. We think our conscious is very smart, and it is. But your subconscious is the genius. When you activate that, it's amazing what happens.

Now, the Conscious process has four functions – we call it the Thought Process. One function is what we call Perception through our senses. Before birth, some of your senses are activated. Balance is, sound is, temperature is. Then after birth, others get added. You take the information that you perceive and you store the information on the Subconscious level. This is what we call memory, caused by chemical changes that take place in the neurons of our brain.

The information that we have learned in books, experienced in our life, conversations, all of that information is stored in the neurons of your brain, never to be lost, never to be forgotten. That stored information is called "the truth." It is also called "reality." We have already learned that our reality, or truth, is incomplete.

Now the second function of the Conscious is that of Association. An association simply means that as you perceive a person or a situation, you're asking yourself the question, "Have I seen anything like this before?" You drop into your Subconscious, which is this huge database that you use to define You. If you have something stored from experience, it becomes meaningful. If you don't have anything stored, the perception is meaningless.

But you also have an emotional stored history in your Subconscious. And sometimes from an embarrassment, or ridicule, sometimes through being scolded, hurt, ashamed, that is there, never to be lost; unless you fix it.

The third function of the conscious is that of Evaluation. Evaluation is asking yourself the question, "What is this that I am looking at or experiencing probably leading me toward?" "What is this probably leading me to?" Something good or something harmful? Something positive or something negative? You are evaluating the probabilities of what you are experiencing. The accuracy of your judgment has a lot to do with your stored reality.

The fourth function of the Conscious is Decision-making, and you are making decisions about your

THOUGHT PATTERNS FOR A SUCCESSFUL CAREER®
Mastering the Attitude of Success™ • Participant Manual
©The Pacific Institute®, LLC

future, not based on what can be, but what has been. And it all happens in a split second! Most of the results you get will always be based, not upon what can be, but what has been.

Dropping to the Subconscious, we already know that we store our "truth" or "reality" about who we know we are here. The Subconscious also handles everything that is automatic for us, as well as our Habits and Attitudes.

I'm going to come over to the Creative Subconscious, which turns out to be a self-regulating mechanism. The creative subconscious has four functions. The first one is to maintain sanity, or what you and I refer to as reality. This Creative Subconscious needs to make sure you behave consistently with what you know to be true – about you.

Subconsciously, because we don't realize this is happening, the Creative Subconscious is constantly comparing what we are doing and how we are acting against that vast historical database in our Subconscious. If the pictures don't match, the Creative Subconscious releases energy and creativity to get us back to "normal" for us. It expands our awareness of other options and opportunities. So when you activate that on purpose, instead of reacting to a situation, it is amazing what happens.

And finally, our teleological nature – our ability to focus in on goals – seems to be a natural part of the Creative Subconscious' need to make the pictures match.

You correct for mistakes based upon not your potential, but the reality you have stored. What kind of a student are you? "I'm a C student," or "I'm a C plus student," or "I'm an A student," or "I'm a D student." How are you at this subject? "I'm average or I'm a C, whatever." What happens to a person who knows they're a C student and for some reason they get an A in a test? If what I'm saying is true, the A is a mistake. Do you know what you tell yourself? "Now I don't need to study for two tests and I can still get my C." Am I right? You can't make yourself study. Why? Because you believe you are a C student.

Now, if you're a C student and get an F on a test (provided that's how you grade) and you know you're a C student, if somebody says, "Let's go out this weekend," what do you say? You're going to say, "I can't go out. I've got to study all weekend so I can pass my test and get an A." How come? "So I can get my C."

Now, why don't you get an A all the time? "Because I'm a C student." You don't do it consciously. You do it subconsciously. Once you establish what's normal for you, once you establish how you are, that process in the creative subconscious makes sure you stay pretty close to behaving like yourself. If you do worse, you correct up. But if you do better than you think you are, you correct down.

Remember, we act in accordance, we behave in accordance, with the truth as we believe it to be, about ourselves, our abilities, the situations we find ourselves in.

SUMMARY: Application

Look at his picture. What is it? It is a picture of a familiar subject. Can you see it?

Remember the thought process and how we take in information. We Perceive, Associate, Evaluate, and make Decisions. We Perceive through our senses and bounce those perceptions off of our stored reality (our past experiences) with a question, "Have I seen anything like this before?" You are looking for associations in your memory.

So, back to the picture. If you are by yourself, you're stuck with your own perception. Therefore your association, evaluation and ultimate decision of what the picture represents is completely dependent upon your own perception. If you are part of a bigger group, you may get insights from others as to what they think it is. This gives you potentially more options to evaluate and help you to come to a more enlightened decision.

If you are stuck, and still not sure what it is that you are looking at, let's demonstrate how smart you really are. How? By improving your focus. By offering you more clarity, you will see answers/solutions that you might not have thought possible. In fact, you will see the solution in a matter of seconds.

THOUGHT PATTERNS FOR A SUCCESSFUL CAREER®
Mastering the Attitude of Success™ • Participant Manual
©The Pacific Institute®, LLC

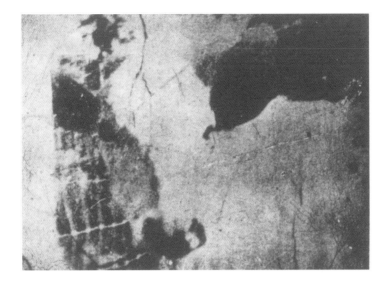

What you are looking at in this picture, is a common farm animal, a cow. In order to see the cow more clearly, it may be easier when the card is turned. Do you see the cow, yet? If you haven't, let's improve your focus a little further. You are looking at the face of a cow, so look for two eyes, two ears, and the long snout. Do you see her now?

Amazing isn't it? Your focus improved with a clear and defined picture. Once you knew specifically what you were looking for, you were able to shift your perspective, look for a specific association, and re-evaluate the image. You began to match the picture on the card with the dominant picture of the face of a cow in your brain until there she was. The more vivid the picture, the more you are drawn toward it.

Be very clear about your intention to get your education and how you intend to use those skills in your new career. You can make your future happen, and it is not so very different from this exercise.

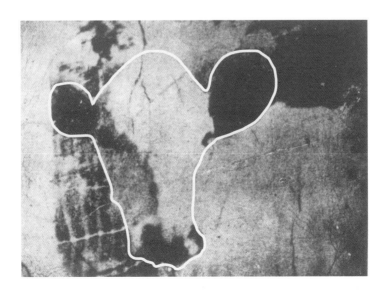

PROCESS OF THOUGHT

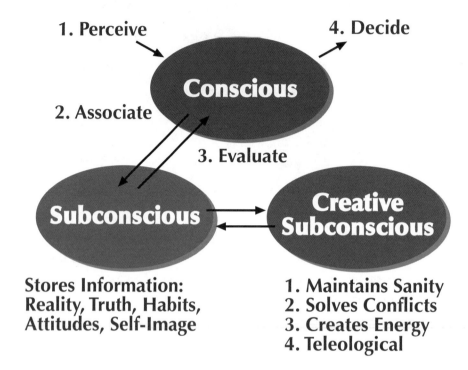

1. Perceive   4. Decide

Conscious

2. Associate

3. Evaluate

Subconscious   **Creative Subconscious**

**Stores Information:
Reality, Truth, Habits,
Attitudes, Self-Image**

**1. Maintains Sanity
2. Solves Conflicts
3. Creates Energy
4. Teleological**

From My Toolbox:
The Reticular Activating System
Sharpening My Focus

OVERVIEW

The human brain has a formation in the central cortex, the Reticular Activating System (RAS), that filters all the information that is bombarding our senses. It only lets through information that is important to us right now. If it let everything through, we could not cope with the chaos! We can put the RAS to work for us, by setting clear, concise goals, so that the necessary information gets through to us when we need it.

OBJECTIVES

By the end of this unit, I will understand:

- I need to know what I am looking for.

- by setting out what is of value to me, I can expand my awareness of the resources that are available to me.

- I must take accountability for my own future.

I am in control of my own future.

LouTice

KEY CONCEPTS

Accountable/Accountability: Responsible; answerable for an outcome.

Reticular Activating System (RAS): A network of neurons in the brainstem involved in consciousness, regulation of breathing; the transmission of sensory stimuli to higher brain centers; a primary alert to awareness network that may function differently in varying degrees of consciousness.

Threat: Words or actions that frighten or imperil.

Value(s): Quality of worth, merit; custom or ideal that people desire as an end or means in and of itself; something of excellence or importance.

THOUGHT PATTERNS FOR A SUCCESSFUL CAREER®
Mastering the Attitude of Success™ • Participant Manual
©The Pacific Institute®, LLC

NOTES

Write down your ideas, observations and insights as you work through this unit. Date your entries.

....

....

....

....

....

....

....

....

....

....

....

....

....

....

....

....

....

....

....

....

REFLECTIVE QUESTIONS

1. What do I intend to get out of my education, as a whole?

   my goal is to complete this chapter of my education. Earning a degree will allow me the freedom to chose where I want to work.

2. What do I intend to get out of each individual class?

3. These are examples of where my RAS has lead me to what I needed:

4. Where in my personal life have I given up accountability to another?

THOUGHT PATTERNS FOR A SUCCESSFUL CAREER®
Mastering the Attitude of Success™ • Participant Manual
©The Pacific Institute®, LLC

EXERCISE: Stuck in Traffic

Have you ever been stuck in traffic on a freeway or turnpike?

Suppose you are on a crowded expressway on your way to meet with your boss and your most important client at noon to close a big deal. It's 10:45 AM, and you're one hour away from the restaurant meeting place. It's raining and the sky is dark.

All of a sudden, the traffic gridlocks.

There's been an accident. Up ahead, a tanker lies on its side across three lanes. From the ruptured tank, oil gushes all over the pavement.

In the middle lane where you are, you're surrounded by idling cars and trucks. There's a divider wall on the left and the shoulder on the right is crammed with emergency vehicles.

Would you make it to your appointment?

Now we'll alter the scenario somewhat.

What if I told you that, at that meeting, your boss had a cashier's check for one million dollars, in your name, provided you arrive in time for the meeting? The check will be torn up at noon, so you have one hour and 15 minutes to get there. Can you do it?

Can you? How might you do it?

The point of all this is that when a desired goal is of sufficient personal value, the resources and action required to reach that goal tend to show up.

EXERCISE: Building a Network

From the list in the left column, take some common obstacles to successfully completing your education. Turn them into resources to manage future obstacles. Allow your RAS to see solutions!

Potential obstacles during my education.	Who do I intend to meet?	Why is it worth my effort to meet them?	What do I need to know about them?	How can they become a resource for any potential obstacles?
Transportation				
Sick child				
Difficulty with course content				
Technical difficulties				
Cash-flow problems				
Lack of family support				

THOUGHT PATTERNS FOR A SUCCESSFUL CAREER®
Mastering the Attitude of Success™ • Participant Manual
©The Pacific Institute®, LLC

EXERCISE: RAS Activity

From List 1, choose one event it would be important for your RAS to find for you. Make it significant to find by the next session of this class. Allow your RAS to find it for you.

- Catch your child(ren) saying "Please" and "Thank you"
- Hear a classmate affirming an answer you give
- Read a job posting in your field
- Hear an instructor affirming a classmate
- Find someone vital to add to your network

From List 2, have fun with your RAS and prove that it works by selecting one of the following. Make it significant to find by the next session of this class. Don't actively search for it, but allow your RAS to find it.

- Green pickup truck
- Black and white cow
- Parking place on a busy street or a busy mall parking lot
- Your favorite coffee shop in an unfamiliar part of town
- Billboard promoting a performer you like

Circle your choices.

Where did you see them? _____

When (date and time) did you see them? _____

What were the conditions? _____

SUMMARY: Fundamentals

Earlier we talked about how our Conscious mind acts as The Great Perceptor, soaking up all the information that is bombarding our senses 24/7/365. The Conscious mind is always on duty.

Now, if we had to pay attention to every little piece of information coming in, it would be chaos. We couldn't move, speak, think clearly, sleep or function at all! What we need is some kind of filter system, to keep the sensory overload down to a bare minimum.

Luckily, our brains provide this service with an actual net-like grouping of cells, at the base of the brain, in the Central Cortex. We call it the Reticular Activating System, or RAS for short. It acts like a good executive secretary, keeping out the interruptions to a CEO's day.

Now, how does the RAS know what information to let through and what information to keep out? Well, we decide what is important – you and I. And what is important? Anything that is of Value or a Threat, right now.

It's like the example of a mother asleep at night, with a small baby nearby. The mother could sleep through trucks rumbling down the road, airplanes flying directly overhead, and never wake up. But if that baby makes the slightest cry, snap! She's awake. You see, it isn't the volume of the sound that wakes her up. It is the importance of her baby's cry. It is tremendously valuable information, because her baby might need the mother.

Lou Tice used to tell the story of a sheriff in a small mid-west town, where it was typical for one of the local bars to have fights. Now, bar fights are pretty noisy affairs, but the simple sound of a shell being loaded into the chamber of a shotgun was enough to stop any fight. Why? Because the next sound that would be heard would be the gun going off, and nobody wanted to be in the way of a shotgun shell!

Value and Threat – that's what gets through our RAS. And who decides what is valuable and what is a threat? You do.

A fun thing to try, if you're looking for a parking spot in a busy part of town, is tell yourself exactly where you want to park. Watch: as you drive down the street, your Reticular Activating System is looking for information. It sees heads in cars two blocks away. It sees people approaching cars. It sees red lights flashing. Those aren't parking spots. Those are clues that lead you to your goal. You set your mind for what's important to you, and now you're scanning. But instead of looking for parking spots, I want you to look for opportunity, for education or information, or for jobs. You can even look for a spouse. That would be all right. You need to be clear, in your mind, what you're looking for, or anything will do. And you don't want just anything.

On the way home today, try this: When you're driving home, tell yourself you want to see every green car with license plates that have a 4 and an H on the plate. You can be going 60 miles an hour, and "There's one, there's one, there's one!" That's how smart you are. And then you take that skill and go after what you want in your life.

This is extremely helpful information, because we can put our RAS to work for us every time we set a new goal. Remember how we talked about the Creative Subconscious opens up our Awareness? The RAS is what we use to increase our awareness of information we need. We use the RAS to bust scotomas that are holding us back.

By setting goals, we are declaring a new priority for our minds to focus on, and our RAS is so good that it immediately begins the search for the information we need.

SUMMARY: Application

The RAS, the Reticular Activating System, inside you and me is our filter system. It lets in threats and it lets in value. So let's talk about the value of attending a class. This is why preparation ahead of time is so important – especially when we were kids, when the teacher asked us to read a chapter ahead of time, because they were punishing us. If we read the chapter ahead, if we looked at the questions ahead of time, if we looked at yesterday's notes (or the day before's notes) ahead of time, it engaged our brain on the priorities, the things deemed important by the teacher. So, when they came up in class, we were better focused – we are better focused – and we hear them and don't miss them.

Another element to this is resources. When we talk about resources, we mean things that we may need to solve obstacles and problems as we navigate our way through our education. When we get to know classmates, and other people around us – even other people in the building, staff and administration – they become resources. When we have a need, all of a sudden our RAS searches and finds the resources for us.

The job of the RAS is to connect the gaps between what we know, and what we need to know, in order to complete projects, and classwork, and assignments or just to get to school. If, all of a sudden, I find I have a transportation problem, because I have gotten to know people, because we have had discussions, I know that someone could actually have the solution to my transportation problem.

It's not magic. It is knowing where you want to go. When we have problems or challenges, the RAS goes to work to fill the gap.

NOTES

4 The "Truth" is What We Believe It Is
Our Beliefs Define Us

OVERVIEW

That picture we hold of ourselves in our subconscious gives us a standard at which we regulate our behavior. This picture, this definition, of who we are – our thoughts and feelings – make up our beliefs, the "truth" about us. The creative subconscious makes sure that we behave in accordance with the picture. Our beliefs are the fuel that drives the engine that is us.

OBJECTIVES

By the end of this unit, I will understand:

- I regulate my behavior at my belief level.

- how to recognize when I'm above or below my standard of what is good enough for me.

- I must change the picture of what is good enough, in order to live and perform to my potential.

We self-regulate at the level of our beliefs,
not at the level of our potential.

LouTice

KEY CONCEPTS

Belief(s): An emotional acceptance of a proposition, statement, or doctrine.

Conscious: The aspect of mind that encompasses all that one is momentarily aware of; that is, those aspects of mental life that one is attending to.

Sanction: To give approval to; to agree with.

Creative Subconscious: The source of mental processes that leads to solutions, ideas, conceptualizations, artistic forms, theories, or products that are unique and novel. A self-regulating mechanism.

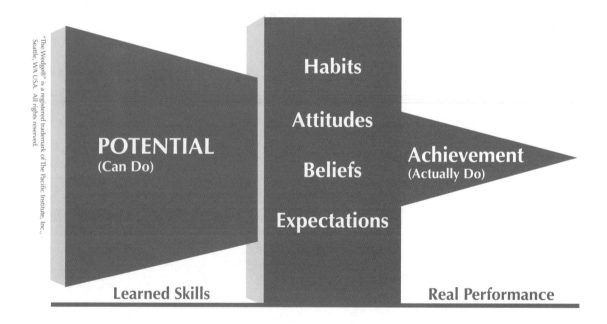

THOUGHT PATTERNS FOR A SUCCESSFUL CAREER®
Mastering the "Attitude of Success"™ • Participant Manual
©The Pacific Institute®, LLC

NOTES

Write down your ideas, observations and insights as you work through this unit. Date your entries.

REFLECTIVE QUESTIONS

1. What information from others have I accepted as "fact" regarding my pursuit of an education?

2. From my answers to Question #1, which are really fact and which are only someone else's opinion that I accepted as "fact"?

3. From the information I accepted as fact, but I now know are only opinions, how have I been influenced in my beliefs about what I can do?

4. How will changing these old beliefs help me in getting the education I want, the career I want?

EXERCISE: I Can or I Can't

In the columns below, list the people from your life who have given you "I Can" feedback, and those people who have given you "I Can't" feedback.

I CAN	I CAN'T

- Who did I sanction the most?

- Why did I sanction them?

- How has that affected my internal conversation, either positively or negatively?

EXERCISE: Balance Wheel

1. Please consider the Balance Wheel below as a visual representation of the most important corporation in the world to you, Me Inc. In each of the slotted spokes, please identify the key functional areas of your life that are most important to you. If the sample works, please use it. If not, replace some of the suggestions with key functional areas more appropriate to you.

2. Next, please reflect on your personal satisfaction that you feel currently in your life with regard to each functional area. On a scale of 1 (lowest) to 10 (highest), please place a dot within each key functional area that represents your current satisfaction within that area of your life.

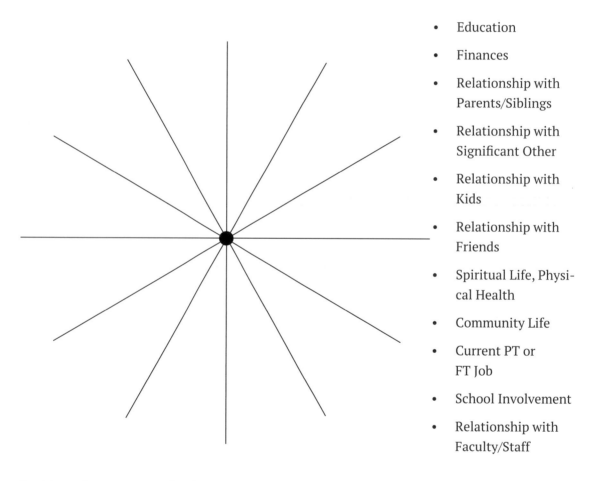

- Education
- Finances
- Relationship with Parents/Siblings
- Relationship with Significant Other
- Relationship with Kids
- Relationship with Friends
- Spiritual Life, Physical Health
- Community Life
- Current PT or FT Job
- School Involvement
- Relationship with Faculty/Staff

3. Next, please connect the dots to your wheel.

   - Does this give you any insights? Are you balanced? How smooth would the ride be if this was a real wheel?

   - In the areas of your Balance Wheel that are most important to you, what truths or beliefs have you sanctioned that may be holding you back from releasing your true potential?

THOUGHT PATTERNS FOR A SUCCESSFUL CAREER®
Mastering the "Attitude of Success"™ • Participant Manual
©The Pacific Institute®, LLC

EXERCISE: Imagination[2]

Everybody has had embarrassing moments, situations where the negative emotions about school and education are all you seem to remember. For this exercise, in the left-side column, take a moment to list a few of those moments and the negative emotions associated with them. Then, in the right-side column, list scenarios that you could put yourself into that would reverse the negative emotion into a positive one.

NEGATIVE MOMENTS	REPLACEMENT EMOTION/SITUATION
Example: Raised hand to answer question, and forgot what I was going to say. Felt stupid.	During class discussions, make short notes of my thoughts and refer to them with confidence when answering questions.

SUMMARY: Fundamentals

All that information that we have been gathering about ourselves, since we were very little, has been stored in our Subconscious and our Subconscious is like a hard drive that cannot be erased. Now, how did we get all that information in the first place? Well, we got it from the look of the house we grew up in; we got it from the neighborhood. A lot of it we got from the people who were, and probably still are, important to us – our parents, brothers and sisters, grandparents, teachers and coaches.

The challenge with all of this information we accepted, or gave sanction to, we took in and labeled "Fact." What we didn't realize is that most of these "facts" were actually only opinions. But once we accept these opinions, they might as well be facts because we believe them and they become a part of who we are – how we define ourselves.

Studies have shown that the ages of 3 to 5 are critical in our acceptance of information coming our way, all the way up to age 11. This is sometimes referred to as the "First 4000 Days." And most of the information we get is from those people closest to us, with their opinions that we take as fact. And facts are pretty difficult to change.

As we learned in the first unit, once we lock on to one way of thinking, we lock out – or build a scotoma to – anything that doesn't match. We just don't see it. This is also our Creative Subconscious making sure we stay the same, reinforcing "reality" or "sanity" for us. This can be beneficial if we know we are forgetful. We don't have to wake up every morning, and remember to remind ourselves we are forgetful. We are just forgetful!

So, are we stuck with these beliefs forever? Not if we don't want to be. You see, at the very foundation of our beliefs are our thoughts. Our thoughts accumulate to become beliefs. So, if we change our thoughts, then we should be able to change our beliefs. We can write over those old files on our hard drive, and get more effective results from our thought process searches.

And once we change our beliefs, then the behaviors that are reflections of those beliefs will change as well.

One last piece: You know how important the self-concept is, the self-image is. I'm going to show you how it's created, and then I'm going to keep showing you how to change it. Have you ever seen anybody under hypnosis, watch it on TV or anything like that? Under hypnosis you go past the Conscious right into the Subconscious. I would just tell you that this chart weighed 500 pounds. So, under hypnosis you'd probably believe that. Once I get you convinced it's the truth, that it weighs 500 pounds, I'd say "I'll give you a thousand dollars if you just come over and pick it up." It would be worth a try, wouldn't it, for a thousand dollars? So, you come, and you try to lift this with your arms, and it won't come up. Now, why won't it come up? It doesn't weigh more than about 4 or 5 pounds.

If we attached electrodes to your biceps, we might show that you're lifting with 75 pounds of energy up, and this only weighs 5 pounds, and it won't come up. Tell me, why is it staying down? Now watch, sanity is more important than being successful, having a good relationship, having a good future, having people treat you well. Sanity is more important. Sanity means what I know to be true needs to happen in my life all the time. If it doesn't, my Creative Subconscious corrects for mistakes. Got it?

Now, I know I'd get a thousand dollars if I lift this, but I believe it weighs 500 pounds. I'm lifting and we're measuring 75 pounds of energy. It still stays down. Here's why: My brain, my Creative Subconscious, sends a message to the muscles at the back of my arm called my triceps that I use for pushing. So, while I'm lifting with my biceps for a thousand dollars, without knowing it (I have a scotoma) I'm pushing with the muscles at the back of my arm. I'm pushing with at least 75 pounds of energy down. I'm doing what's called an isometric contraction. I'm lifting and pushing at the same time. But I don't know I'm pushing. All I know is how hard I'm working.

If you ever work "real hard" at something with no results, change your mind about how good you are, whether it's hard, or what you're capable of. Because what you'll do is you'll try hard, try hard, try hard, with no success and just get frustrated. The process between the Subconscious and the Creative Subconscious always tries to make "the truth" happen.

So, your job is to do what? Change the truth.

There is one more vital piece of information that you need to know: We think in pictures. Let me prove it to you. Close your eyes. What do you see when I say the word "apple"? OK, now what do you see when I say, "green apple"? Did your picture change? Our beliefs are just that easy to change.

SUMMARY: Application

It was the 10th grade. I'm walking into Algebra II/Accelerated. Now, how did I wind up in Algebra II/Accelerated – algebra with the "smart kids"? Somehow, someway, I had proven to be worthy of this class. As I was walking into the class, I looked off to my right, and there was Mr. M – 6'2", 215 pounds and a former Marine. Sculpted, intimidating stature of a man. He crooked his finger at me and said, "I've been waiting for you."

So, I approached him and he pointed to a desk, right in front of him, and said, "That will be your seat." See, Mr. M was going to take care of me. He had had my father as a teacher, and I do believe he liked my dad.

As the class started, I was having difficulty in this class, to say the least. But I had certain HABEs (habits, attitudes, beliefs and expectations) inside of me. You see, my parents were both teachers, so the HABEs I had gotten from both of them was, I really understood the role of a teacher. And I understood my expectations of being a good student was getting good grades. So, when Mr. M started to teach, and I didn't understand, I would raise my hand. See, when my father taught me "there are no dumb questions," I believed him. If you believe "there are no dumb questions," then you have a tendency to ask.

So, I would ask the question, and what would happen is that Mr. M would move to his next teaching technique: he would approach my desk, get as close as he could, and then he would say the same thing, a little bit louder. I'm starting to get a little bit intimidated by the approach, but I still have a problem: I don't understand. Because of the HABEs inside of me, I'm trying to figure out whether or not I asked the question correctly. Maybe he didn't understand what I don't understand, so therefore, I tried to figure out another way of asking.

Mr. M, because I am asking the same question again – just maybe a little differently – is getting a little bit more frustrated with me. So now, he would answer the question – in my perception pretty much the same way – but now he would whip chalk off the sides of the room. So, now there is exploding chalk off of the side walls of the room, in answer to my question.

This whole scene is now starting to bring on a little attention from the other students in class, so I'm starting to feel a little bit more uncomfortable. At the same time, I've got a growing problem here. Just because Mr. M is now yelling and whipping chalk at the walls, does not mean that I understand better now, or that I understand and am going to be OK. I still didn't understand.

For the life of me, and why I did this I don't know, but I raised my hand – again. This time, it was the final, killing blow for me. "Get to the board!" A healthy dose, from Mr. M, of embarrassment and humiliation, in front of a classroom full of my peers. I still get that warm feeling today.

I believed I no longer did math. I no longer did algebra. I just went into survival mode. It wasn't about learning anymore, it was about passing the class. It was about doing what I needed to do, just to get by. But because of that experience, how did it influence my academic career? At the end of the year, when I met with my guidance counselor, Mr. S says to me, "Scott, you are college prep material. You going to college?" Yes sir. "So what math are you taking?" No sir. He looked at me and said, "Scott, you need to take geometry to graduate from high school." So I said, fine give me geometry, because I do expect to graduate from high school. So, I got straight C's in geometry. I didn't have very high expectations for myself.

The next year, I was wise. When I walked down to talk with the counselor, he said, "Scott, you are college prep material." Yes sir. "What math are you taking?" No sir. I listened last year. I don't care if you give me a study hall, I'm not taking another math! But he said, "Scott, aren't you going to college?" Oh, yes sir! "You are going to have to take math there." Yes sir, and I will worry about it then! Why in the world would I willingly put myself into a situation that I don't have to?

That experience, there is no question, greatly affected my belief in myself, of what I was capable of doing. But honestly, I was as much a contributor as the teacher. Just because I didn't see it the same way that Mr. M was teaching it, it was my perception and what I locked onto about what I couldn't do, that held me back. Therefore, if I wanted to change it, it was up to me. Trust me, just like many of you, I still had math to take in the future.

5

My Internal Conversation – 24/7/365

The Constant Conversation I Have with Myself

OVERVIEW

Our thoughts accumulate to become beliefs, so it is vitally important to control our thoughts. We do this by controlling our self-talk, that constant conversation that goes on in our minds. This self-talk is essential in forming our self-image, and can either build us up or tear us down. In fact, understanding the power of self-talk may be the most important thing we can ever learn.

OBJECTIVES

By the end of this unit, I will understand:

- that my beliefs are formed by the way that I talk to myself.

- what others tell me won't become a part of me unless I give sanction or agree with it.

- groups of people, large or small, have their own self-talk, and it is reflected in outward performance.

We build our own reality with our own thoughts.

LouTice

KEY CONCEPTS

Sanction: To give approval to; to agree with

Self-Talk: An act whereby one evaluates or assesses one's behavior; how one talks or reaffirms to oneself when one reacts to one's own evaluation, or others' evaluations of one's performance. Self-talk may have an affirming influence in establishing self-image.

The next time . . .: A vow to better performance at the next opportunity.

NOTES

Write down your ideas, observations and insights as you work through this unit. Date your entries.

REFLECTIVE QUESTIONS

1. In what areas of my life has my self-talk been very negative? In what areas has it been much more positive?

2. When I speak to those I care about, do I spend most of my time pointing out the things they do wrong, or what they do right?

3. How might I create an environment with my family, friends, classmates, or colleagues, where we focus on the positive and spend less time focusing on the negative?

THOUGHT PATTERNS FOR A SUCCESSFUL CAREER®
Mastering the Attitude of Success™ • Participant Manual
©The Pacific Institute®, LLC

EXERCISE: Fact or Opinion

For the list of sources in the middle of the table below, check whether you think information coming from these sources is "Fact" or "Opinion." Prepare to defend your choices.

FACT	SOURCES	OPINION
	Newspapers	
	Television News	
	Social Networking Websites	
	Weekly Newsmagazine	
	Dictionary	
	Your Instructor	
	Blogosphere	
	Tweets	
	Electric Service Invoice	
	History Text	
	Religious Text	
	Doctor's Prognosis	
	Math Text	
	Astronomy Picture of the Day	
	Wikipedia	

EXERCISE: Self-Talk and My Moods

Read the story on this page then answer the questions below the story. Do the same with the story on the next page.

MISSING DOG REUNITED WITH OWNER

Three years is a long time to be gone, but Titan recognized his owner immediately with a lot of jumping and wiggling. "I always thought he was still alive [but] after all this time, I had given up," said Titan's owner.

As a two-year-old, Titan had somehow escaped from a fenced-in backyard, and despite his owner contacting the local animal shelters and veterinarian offices, was never found. The only conclusion was that someone had picked up Titan, and kept him.

Three years later, a family brought the dog into a local pet re-homing organization, hoping to find another home for the dog. It seems Titan had continued his escape-artist ways, and the family could not handle him anymore. The dog was scanned for a microchip implant. The chip was found, but it had migrated down into one of Titan's legs, far from the original insertion point. A call was made to Titan's original owner.

"I was so surprised by the call," said Titan's owner. "Nothing I expected after all this time." Titan was picked up the next day, with a lot of happy wiggling and jumping around. A representative for the shelter relayed, "It is thrilling to be able to reunite lost pets with their owners. This is definitely one of our happiest stories and we were so happy to bring the pair back together."

1. What's your initial response to the story about Titan? What was your self-talk like as you read the story?

2. How long is too long to hold onto a hope/goal/dream?

3. Have you ever wanted to give up?

4. What encourages you to persist toward that hope/goal/dream?

THOUGHT PATTERNS FOR A SUCCESSFUL CAREER®
Mastering the Attitude of Success™ • Participant Manual
©The Pacific Institute®, LLC

EXERCISE: Self-Talk and My Moods, cont.

Read the story on this page then answer the questions below the story.

STORM POUNDS N. CALIFORNIA WITH RAIN AND HIGH WINDS

A powerful winter storm slammed into Northern California causing power outages to thousands of homes and businesses as well as traffic delays throughout the greater Bay area. Flights were delayed or cancelled at San Francisco International Airport, ferries were bound to their docks, and travel across the Golden Gate Bridge was a challenge as high winds caused cars to swerve out of lanes.

Although there were multiple accidents on flooded roads and highways, there were no initial reports of serious injuries. An elementary school student was trapped for about 15 minutes under a fallen tree until rescuers with chain saws cut the tree apart. He was taken to the hospital with a possible broken arm. "It's a two-pronged punch. It's wind and rain. Once the ground gets saturated and the winds are howling, there's a bigger chance of trees going down on power lines," said a National Weather Service spokesperson.

Forecasters warn the impact could get worse. Mudslides are possible, especially in areas affected by this year's wildfires, and with as much as 8 inches of rain falling, rivers and creeks were rising fast. Northern Californians were warned days in advance of the coming storm, and many got ready. By Wednesday night some stores announced they had run out of water, batteries and flashlights, and some cities tweeted that they had no sandbags or sand left.

1. How did this story make you feel?

2. What was your self-talk like as you read the story?

3. Have you ever been in an extreme situation such as this?

4. Typically, what is your first response to stressful situations that are beyond your control?

Ultimately, we must control our self-talk or our self-talk will control us. It is important to bring our self-talk to conscious awareness, especially when it is running us down.

EXERCISE: Moods: By Accident or Intent?

There is significant research on the power of our self-talk to affect our moods. So, rather than leave our moods to chance, or react to the world around us, we can be proactive. We can be deliberate and intentional.

Take 30 seconds to write down as many of your favorite things as you can think of – people, places, foods, music, activities, whatever makes you happy.

_____

_____

_____

_____

_____

_____

_____

_____

_____

_____

_____

_____

_____

Place this list on your nightstand or bathroom mirror. Begin each day by reading through your list. Take a few moments to reflect and remember those good, positive feelings.

After a week, do you look forward to reading your list? Do the memories make you smile?

Observe your self-talk. Has it been more positive?

Have your attitudes and reactions to situations changed? Have they been more positive?

SUMMARY: Fundamentals

We have already learned that our thoughts accumulate to become our beliefs, and that our beliefs about ourselves and the world around us have come from a lot of different sources – parents, grandparents, teachers and coaches. And, we have also learned that because of our beliefs, we are not seeing everything there is to see, hearing everything there is to hear – in short, we know we build scotomas because of our beliefs.

One more reminder: We think in pictures, triggered by the words we use or hear or think. And, we add emotions to those pictures, based on what has happened to us in the past. All of this is stored in our subconscious to become our reality – our strongest pictures that define who we think we are, our self-image.

It has been estimated that we have over 50,000 thoughts per day. That's roughly one thought every 1-3/4 seconds! And that's with our RAS keeping out perceptions from our senses that aren't important to us at the moment!

So in the world of psycholinguistics this constant conversation we are having with ourselves is called "meta cognition" – or an easier way to think of it is "self-talk." We are talking with ourselves constantly and while you are listening to me, you are thinking 3 times as fast as I am talking. When I stop talking, you speed up to 6 times faster!

Now, having all these thoughts during the day would be great, if they were positive and reinforcing of a healthy self-image. Unfortunately, for those who haven't learned what you are learning, those thoughts are probably negative, sarcastic and belittling – internally and externally.

We do and say so much without thinking about it, that unconsciously we are reinforcing negative pictures, which cause a lower self-image and leave us feeling "less than" about ourselves, our current situations, and the environment around us. What we want to do is become more aware of what we say to ourselves, and what we hear from others.

So, in the spirit of greater awareness, I am going to give you another test. Don't worry, it is not difficult, but it will be enlightening if you participate with a little attention and enthusiasm. Here goes: For the next 24 hours, you will not speak negatively to yourself, about yourself, or about anyone else. This is the No Negative Self-Talk Test – no sarcasm, no belittling, and no devaluation of yourself or others for 24 hours.

I know what you are thinking: It's going to be mighty quiet around here! It might be, but I'm willing to bet that when this 24 hours is over, you will finally understand how negative your world has become, and how that negativity has affected your level of satisfaction with school or work, your family, and your own happiness.

Now, it is not enough to just be aware of the negativity. If you are like most people, you want to get out of the negativity rut. No one really wants to be unhappy. This is where the flip-side of Self-Talk comes in. Remember Words, Pictures and Emotions? Change the words, which give you different pictures, causing more positive emotions!

Now, the changing of the words needs to be purposeful – it cannot be left to chance. Now that you are aware of the negative self-talk, and you think or say something that is belittling or devaluative, say to yourself, "Stop it! I'm better than that. The next time, I intend to…" and then you tell yourself what you want to do better at the next time. You stop the current behavior, and replace it with a positive picture of the change you want.

I'm going to give you a little formula that will help you create the replacement pictures for your subconscious to use. I x V = R. Imagination times Vividness equals Reality. This works because your subconscious cannot tell the difference between something that actually happens and a vivid picture being created. All it cares about are the pictures. That's why Michael Jordan did all those free throws in his head – his Subconscious didn't know they weren't real. That's why the best golfers see how they want to play a hole before they T-up the ball. Why hockey and soccer players look to the gaps in order to score, and why batters look for where the outfielders aren't so they can hit the ball in the gaps.

Controlling your self-talk is probably the most important lesson I could teach you. It affects every belief and every behavior we play out in our lives. We use self-talk to create new pictures about what we want, and our behaviors follow – as long as those new, replacement pictures are stronger than the way current reality is for us right now. Our subconscious doesn't care which way we go – the old picture, or the new one – it only follows the strongest picture.

Researchers say it takes three weeks to three months to create a new habit. You can use your positive self-talk to move faster and stronger to get you to what you want.

SUMMARY: Application

Thoughts accumulate to form beliefs. Once you learn this discipline, it will change your life forever. The discipline is controlling your self-talk.

A teacher walks into a Kindergarten classroom and asks, who in here is an artist? How many kids raise their hands? Most likely, all of them. Why?

How did this happen? A child draws a picture, mom or dad says it's beautiful, and we have a positive thought for the child. Then mom hangs the artwork on the refrigerator, another positive thought for the child. Mom or Dad doesn't have to keep telling the child how wonderful it is. The child just has to recall it with his own self-talk. Every time he recalls the wonderful comments about his artwork with his own self-talk, it's like it's happening again. Then, the child walks past the refrigerator, looks at the artwork, there it is again. That's mine, he affirms it again with his own self-talk. Thinks about mom making such a big deal about it, it happens again. Then Grandma comes over and looks at the artwork on the refrigerator. "Who did this? Can I have it? You didn't sign it, every great artist signs his work. I'm going to put it in a frame and place it on my mantle." Again, another positive affirmation from the outside. He internalizes it, sanctions it, repeats it with his own self-talk, again and again and again.

But before Grandma can take the picture to her house, older brother walks by and sees the artwork. "What is it? That's stupid! You didn't even stay in the lines! You can't draw. You can't color."

Even out of the mouth of a three-year-old, he may size up older brother and say, "Oh yeah, well Grandma loves it!" In other words, I sanction Grandma more than I sanction you.

We cannot control what the world has to say, but we can control what we have to say to ourselves. Thoughts accumulate to form beliefs. In areas where I think well of myself, chances are my own thoughts have allowed me to release the talents inside of me because of how I have built myself up with my own self-talk. But in other areas, what have I sanctioned, then kept pulling myself down with my own negative self-talk? It's time to reverse the process in those areas.

NOTES

6

What Can I Make Happen for Me?
Increasing My Causative Power

OVERVIEW

Self-efficacy is our belief in what we can cause, bring about or make happen – the higher the efficacy, the higher the causative power inside of us. Our efficacy appraisal, positive or negative, is attached to our emotional history. These are real feelings, real emotions, that are not always connected to an actual truth, but to what we believe to be true. As we continue to grow, our beliefs need to be challenged, and some may need to be changed.

OBJECTIVES

By the end of this unit, I will understand:

- my self-efficacy is my estimation of what I believe I can cause.

- the impact my self-efficacy has on what I allow myself to do.

- when I shy away from a project, it is because my self-efficacy is low.

- raising my own self-efficacy will help those around me to raise theirs.

Our self-efficacy is our belief in what we can cause, bring about, and make happen for ourselves and the world around us.

KEY CONCEPTS

Self-Efficacy: One's appraisal of one's own ability to cause, to bring about, make happen; one's own power or capacity to produce the desired effect; a combination of one's self-esteem, skills, and resources; task specific.

Self-Image: The accumulation of all the attitudes and opinions one has perceived about oneself that form a subconscious picture of oneself; the imagined self; the self that one supposes oneself to be; the picture; self-regulation.

Humility: A trait characterized by lack of pretense.

NOTES

Write down your ideas, observations and insights as you work through this unit. Date your entries.

REFLECTIVE QUESTIONS

1. In what areas of my life is my self-efficacy high?

2. In what areas of my life is my self-efficacy low?

3. Where my self-efficacy is low, what are my beliefs about those areas?

4. Moving forward, what do I want those beliefs to be, so that I can raise my self-efficacy for me and for my loved ones?

THOUGHT PATTERNS FOR A SUCCESSFUL CAREER®
Mastering the Attitude of Success™ • Participant Manual
©The Pacific Institute®, LLC

EXERCISE: Building My Self-Efficacy

On the lines below, list 10 things that you have done well in your life to date:

- _____
- _____
- _____
- _____
- _____

- _____
- _____
- _____
- _____
- _____

Choose one or two of your own examples from the list above. Think carefully about each situation and determine the evidence that allows you to see your part in the achievements.

- What was your self-talk like, as your efficacy grew?

- How did you handle any obstacles or challenges that happened along the way?

- How did you persist when "nay-sayers" told you it was not possible?

- Who did you listen to? Who were the people whose words you sanctioned?

- How did the people you sanctioned help or hurt your self-efficacy in this instance?

EXERCISE: Adding Positive Weights

- Think about coaching another student into reaching his/her potential

- What would you do or say to influence their attitude? Help them to create habits? Increase their efficacy? Make sure they don't miss anything?

Think of a specific event or task.	What would you do/ say to increase his/her efficacy?	What "evidence" of their growth would you make certain he/she sanctions from you?	What would you do/ say to influence his/her attitude?
EXAMPLE: Helping my child learn her multiplication tables	1. Use flash cards 2. Keep 2 separate piles (correct and incorrect answers) 3. At the completion of all the cards, show her how many she got correct. 4. As we repeat the activity and the correct pile grows, keep reinforcing the fact that the "correct" pile continues to grow and she is causing it.	• Homework grades improving • Test scores going up • Any comments or affirmations from the teacher • The "correct" pile growing as she does her flash cards	• Be sure to tell her how proud I am about her hard work and subsequent growth • Hang homework papers and test scores on the refrigerator • Ask her how she feels when she sees the high grades • In front of her, tell her grandparents, and other significant people in her life about how hard she is working to learn her multiplication tables and how proud I am of her effort

SUMMARY: Fundamentals

According to Dr. Albert Bandura, self-efficacy is a person's belief in his or her ability to succeed in a particular situation. Bandura described these beliefs as causes behind how we think, behave, and feel. It is my appraisal, my personal assessment of what I think I can cause.

Why is self-efficacy important? When we set a goal, we internally make an efficacy appraisal about whether or not we can see ourselves causing it, or making it happen. The higher the efficacy, the greater the willingness that you will take on the challenge, put yourself in the situation, and keep working until you get it right. Most of that appraisal has to do with our historical memories of events or situations or similar goals and my perception of that outcome as compared to the new goal.

If it was a positive experience, the successful completion of the goal, something that I know that I am good at, then I most likely will project those positive feelings and high efficacy, my high causative power, into achieving the new goal.

But if it was a negative experience, then most likely I will project just the opposite and come to a quick conclusion: "Why try? We know how this turned out the last time we tried this. Let's save ourselves the embarrassment and humiliation and forget about it." And even if you do get yourself to try, you are probably not "all in." The Creative Subconscious, inside of you, has the job of maintaining you as you are, not as you can be. So, it is secretly planning your way out, compiling all the reasons as to why this new goal won't work. So, when you are ready to bail, the excuses are there to come to your rescue.

The dreams you have are in direct proportion to how good you think you are. Out of Stanford University, by Dr. Albert Bandura, who is the best in the world in the research of this, said to me one time, "We don't let ourselves want what we don't believe we can cause," even though the potential is inside of ourselves. What does he mean by that?

Well, I was a high school teacher and had taken the vow of poverty by mistake. I mean, we were poor. The cars we were driving were junk heaps. Just wrecks. Every summer we'd say, "We've got to get a new car." Now listen to that statement: a "new" car. I wasn't even thinking of a new car. Do you know what I was thinking? A new junk heap. I didn't think a new car and back it up to a junk heap. A new car never came to my mind. How big you dream isn't because of your potential; it's because of your appraisal of how good you are.

When you set a goal, the question of efficacy in your mind is this: is this goal bigger than me right now or am I bigger than it? Can I pull it off? Do I know how to do it? Do I have the knowledge? Do I have the skill? Do I have the money to buy it? Do I have the money to create the business I want? Do I have the ability to take the courses I want to get the job I want to get the degree I want?

If you start to feel scared, subconsciously, you start backing away from the goal. You start backing up the goal. You start creating negative avoidance inside your mind. You start telling yourself, "Oh, my gosh, I will lose everything. I'll be embarrassed." You wake up at 2:00 in the morning with, "It won't work. It won't work!" When people set a goal bigger than their present capability, if they don't know any better, they become sensible. They become realistic, and back up the goal. "Let's be sensible about this." What does that mean to most people? It means don't set a goal bigger than what you presently know how to do. You're not qualified.

Here's what I want you to do: Set the goals beyond your present capability, always. Set your goals outside of your comfort zone. Set your goals based upon what you really love to do. Yes, when you do that you're going to get the tension inside of yourself, but what that does, if you do it right, it causes you to study, to do what it takes to realize the goal.

In order to achieve our new activity, our goal needs to get our attention. It needs to have our focus. Most importantly, we need to keep evaluating our positive progress toward our goal. With each step in the right direction, each positive evaluation, we increase our efficacy.

What is the most important aspect of a major league baseball player getting a hit? Stepping to the plate! Higher efficacy doesn't mean you'll always get a hit, but it does take you into the batter's box.

SUMMARY: Application

Are you a good speller? By asking that question, you are being asked to make an efficacy appraisal. You either see yourself as being able to cause the success of spelling words correctly or not. Well, how did you come to "know" whether or not you are a good speller? Let's go back to your historical memory and the emotions wrapped around your experiences of spelling.

If you always got good grades, other people typically ask you how to spell words, or you performed very well in spelling bees (maybe even won some), you probably think of yourself as a good speller. For the most part, very positive feelings and lots of evidence that shows you are a good speller. Therefore, when asked the question, you probably, automatically responded affirmatively – a positive efficacy appraisal.

But what if you had the opposite experience? You never got good grades, was always the first kid to sit down during the spelling bee, or maybe even got teased and laughed at by the other kids. As each negative experience mounted, you came to dread studying your words. You came to dread test time. Even now, to this day, you are thankful for spell-check so the world won't know how bad a speller you are. So when asked, "Are you a good speller?" you didn't respond affirmatively. Maybe, you even got a little nervous thinking you might be asked to spell something, and you really don't want to do it in front of others!

Spelling probably hasn't cost someone an education. Unfortunately, there have been other classes, other subjects, that have. When you find yourself in that class for you, the one that makes your stomach churn because of all the negative feelings you have associated with that course, remember the importance of efficacy – of being willing to step to the plate to release your potential.

Your efficacy appraisal, positive or negative, is attached to feelings – real feelings and emotions that in some cases may need to be changed. But they are not often attached to real evidence of what you are actually capable of. Let's consider how many words each of us spells on any given day between text messages, tweets, Instagram, emails, social media sites, search engines, class notes, writing papers – it is definitely hundreds, but more than likely thousands of words. Even the worst spellers among us, how many of those words do you think are actually misspelled? 2%? 5%? Maybe 7%? In comparison to the number of words spelled correctly, the number misspelled is relatively small. But when asked if you think you are a good speller, you responded negatively and let the feeling outweigh the evidence.

When you enter a new course or new task with low efficacy, you want to raise it to start getting closer to your actual potential. How? By making sure you see and take ownership of each piece of evidence that you are causing your own learning.

NOTES

....

....

....

....

....

....

....

....

....

....

....

....

....

....

....

....

....

....

....

THOUGHT PATTERNS FOR A SUCCESSFUL CAREER®
Mastering the Attitude of Success™ • Participant Manual
©The Pacific Institute®, LLC

7 My Habits and Attitudes
Labor Saving or Anchors Holding Me Back?

OVERVIEW

There is a great advantage to being able to rely on our habits. We don't need to stop and think about how to do many routine things. However, when those habits keep us stuck in a rut, under-living our potential, we need to see about changing them. In the same manner, our attitudes can limit our achievements. The good news is that habits and attitudes can be changed.

OBJECTIVES

By the end of this unit, I will understand:

- my habits are formed by repetition upon repetition at the conscious level, and then turned over to my subconscious for instant response to situations.

- that in order to change a habit, I first need to realize where I act on autopilot.

- an attitude simply reflects the direction in which I am leaning – toward (positive) or away (negative) – in my thinking.

Keep the goal – just change the habits and attitudes.

LouTice

KEY CONCEPTS

Attitude: A consciously held belief or opinion; easiest to visualize if we picture ourselves leaning toward those things we like (positive) and away from those things we dislike (negative).

Habit: A learned act; a pattern of activity that has, through repetition, become automatic, fixed, and easily and effortlessly carried out.

NOTES

Write down your ideas, observations and insights as you work through this unit. Date your entries.

REFLECTIVE QUESTIONS

1. Where in the past have I intentionally created habits in order to accomplish my goals?

2. If I were to identify one habit to "Undo," what would it be?

3. What are some examples from the past where I gave up on a goal, rather than change my attitude?

EXERCISE: My Habits Inventory

List five (5) Habits that you have developed "by accident," without conscious awareness:

- _____
- _____
- _____

- _____
- _____

List five (5) Habits that you have developed "on purpose," deliberately, and by intent:

- _____
- _____
- _____

- _____
- _____

List five (5) Habits that, if developed consciously (by intent) would guarantee your success in education:

- _____
- _____
- _____

- _____
- _____

List five (5) Habits that, if developed consciously (by intent) would guarantee your career success:

- _____
- _____
- _____

- _____
- _____

EXERCISE: Changing the Habitual Flow...

Think of a class that has you concerned. Work from the bottom up. Now, raise what you expect of yourself, whether it be the final grade, content you will learn, skill you will acquire. What would the belief need to be? What would the attitude need to be? What habituated behaviors would match the new Attitude, Belief and Expectation?

EXAMPLE CHART: Math

Is this sanity?   Is this sanity?

Low Probability of Success	Subject: Math	High Probability of Success
• Skip class • Arrive late • Blow off homework •	4 - Habits • What are the repeated, subconscious behaviors that you intend to apply to this math course?	• Attend • On time • Ask questions • Do homework • Read/Do practice problems
• Negative • Leaning away from, avoidant, "have to"	3 - Attitude • What is your attitude toward math that matches?	• Positive • Leaning toward, engaged, participative, "want to"
• No value • No relevance • Not important • Can't do it!	2 - Beliefs • What is your belief about the math course that matches?	• Has value • Has relevance • Is important • Can do it!
• Low • Boring, too hard, just hope to pass, get out without killing my GPA	1 - Expectations • What do you expect of yourself going into the math course?	• High • To learn, to use these skills in my career • Master the concepts • Get an "A"

Depending upon your level of expectation, your creative subconscious works to line up your habits, attitudes and beliefs appropriately. When faced with a subject or course where you have a history of poor grades or performance, consider how you might consciously adjust your behaviors (upper right box) to more align with a high probability of success.

EXERCISE: Changing the Habitual Flow…

DIRECTIONS: Choose a current class and work through your Expectations, Beliefs, Attitudes and Habits for Low and High Probability of Success.

YOUR CHART:

Low Probability of Success	Subject: _____	High Probability of Success
	4 - Habits	
	3 - Attitude	
	2 - Beliefs	
	1 - Expectations	

EXERCISE: Lifeboat

IMAGINE that the cruise liner on which you have been having the holiday of a lifetime has just sunk, following a devastating explosion in her boilers. With very little time available to save yourself, you now find you are adrift in a lifeboat with other survivors, miles from the nearest land and without the means of contacting the outside world to summon help.

Your lifeboat is totally alone and contains other survivors like yourself. The lifeboat, however, is not quite full and has the capacity to take four more survivors and no more. As time goes by, the lifeboat comes across the following survivors in the water:

- Mother & Child (count as one) ✓
- Liner's First Mate = *not*
- 16-year-old boy (High-dependency drug user)
- 86-year-old woman ✗
- Winner of a reality TV show (A)
- Nurse
- 80 year old survivor of the Asian tsunami disaster ✗
- Secondary-school teacher (A)
- Lone parent
- Foreign national (A)
- Prostitute (A)
- Head of an organized drug consortium 7

NOTES

....

....

....

....

....

....

....

After you have completed your choices, please answer the questions on the following page.

EXERCISE: Lifeboat, cont.

- Did you, or your group, set up a clear and defined goals to determine which survivors would be considered? Was there one main goal, or several?

our goal was to save children first who have not yet experienced life and also to allow

goal — provide survival opportunity to children and parents and person who could care for them.

- Did this help or hurt the decision-making process? If you didn't have a clear and defined goal, would having one have made the decision-making process easier?

- How did any attitudes or initial perceptions toward the survivors influence discussions or the final decisions?

- Once you learned the deeper descriptions of the survivors, how did that affect your attitudes or your reaction to the exercise itself? Did this affect your participation?

SUMMARY: Fundamentals

Habits can emerge outside our consciousness, or can be deliberately designed. In other words, we develop habits by accident and intent. When a habit is created outside of conscious thought, you do it by accident, like cracking your knuckles, chewing your nails, playing with your hair when you are nervous, or using "um" as a transition when speaking. When a habit is created by intent, it is a deliberate action, like athletes, artists, dancers, musicians. How did their actions develop to the point of free-flowing? By the willingness to practice, practice, practice, repeat, repeat, repeat until the action became automatic at a very high level.

Driving a car starts off on the conscious level, and then through repetition and repetition, you turn it over to your subconscious. You don't even think about what you're doing. When you first started driving, probably in the parking lot, you were frozen.

As you learned, everything was sequenced. The right skills, repeated over and over again, allowed you to flow. Even though you couldn't get out of the parking lot, now you can drive down the road, one hand on the wheel, the other one around a girlfriend, looking for people on both sides of the street and looking for cops out of the rearview mirror. You are listening to the radio, you can do it all. There was a time when you couldn't do it all. That's what habits are good for, they let you free flow.

How was it possible for them or for us to create the habit? By having a clearly defined goal, a vivid image of the intention, and a high expectation of the result. Think of all the habits we have in our lives that we have developed by intent: riding a bike, driving a car, playing video games, or mastering the countless apps on our smartphones. Because we desire the result, we are willing to put in the work. So we practice, practice, practice and repeat, repeat, repeat. When we approach behaviors with a want to, choose to, I like it, I love it frame of mind, it is easy to muster all the drive, energy, passion, and motivation we need to develop the habit. Our brain creates it for us because we want it that way.

As the pilot of our lives, we have assimilated feelings, viewpoints, and tendencies in all areas of our lives towards people, places, foods, sports teams, certain subjects in school, things we like, things we don't like. These habituated thought patterns that were repeated over and over until they became automatic, became the attitudes with which we guide our lives.

Have you ever been told you had a bad attitude? Yes? Now, do you know what an attitude is? An attitude is just your emotional history. Remember that perception, association, evaluation and decision making I told you about the conscious level? You see something, and you have a negative attitude. Now, negative doesn't mean bad or wrong; negative means avoidant. Positive doesn't mean good. Positive means you seek out, and try to possess.

The best definition of an attitude I ever found was airplane terminology, like pilots use. If my arms were the wings of an airplane, stretching out to my sides, the attitude of an airplane is just the direction in which the airplane is leaning in relationship to a fixed point like the horizon. So if you just remember, an attitude is just the direction in which you lean.

It all has a lot to do with the emotion that's inside of you. You picked up some emotions when you were three, seven, or 17. You are picking up emotion about what you like and what you don't like about food, about people, about work. With your mind, you're going to perceive something. You associate, "Have I seen anything like this before," and how did I feel about it? Then you say to yourself, evaluative, "What is this probably leading me to?" If it's hurtful, going to embarrass you or make a fool of you, you subconsciously engage in avoidant behavior.

A negative attitude just means moving away. It doesn't mean you're wrong or bad, it just means you move away. If you have a negative attitude about talking in front of people, about certain kinds of classes, or a negative attitude about certain kinds of work or jobs, when you perceive the opportunity to engage in it, you subconsciously figure out why you don't like it. You subconsciously tell yourself why you can't do it. You start to procrastinate, putting it off. When you have a negative attitude, it just makes you take longer to do your homework or do your work.

If you have a negative attitude, you even get yourself sick. You'll want to avoid, subconsciously.

You don't do this consciously. It is that emotional history. When it comes up and it's negative, you get procrastination. Or, you get creative avoidance, and find stuff to do that doesn't need to be done. Instead of doing the stuff you need to do, you find stuff that doesn't need to be done.

Why? Because you don't want to do what you're supposed to do. It's procrastination, creative avoidance, and you just can't get yourself to do it.

Do you know what most people do? They give up on their goal, because they can't get themselves to do the schoolwork or do what's necessary – talk to the people, whatever it might be. You just can't get yourself to do it, and you can't understand why. You might say to yourself, "I was born this way." Well, you may have been born this way, but I doubt it.

Don't give up on what you want you want. Change your attitude.

If the thought of the new goal elicits negative attitudes, we must change the attitude in order to smoothly move into our goal. Therefore, you may want to ask yourself, "Is my present attitude toward attendance, or logging in to my online class, or doing homework, or reading the course materials or participating in class discussion, taking me toward my goal of graduation or away from it?

SUMMARY: Application

In six years of primary school, three years of middle school, three years of high school, four years of undergraduate study, 2.5 years of graduate study, five years of doctoral work, and having spent the better part of the last 25 years working with academic institutions, it's very clear to me that there is one habit that trumps all others when it comes to completing an education. If graduation is important; if you truly desire the new life, the new opportunities that your education will bring to you; there is one habit beyond all others that is paramount to your success. I hope you are very intentional and deliberate about creating it. Whether you are an online or on-ground student, its importance to your success is the same. It is Attendance.

Attendance will make you or break you. Attendance is the ultimate soft skill; it is not a hard skill. It doesn't take aptitude or IQ to decide to show up. Attendance needs to be routinized. It needs to become a habit on the way to your goal of graduation. Attendance needs to become a behavior that you repeat and it doesn't take a conscious decision on your part to make it happen.

Here's the best part: You don't have to keep that picture in front of you forever; just long enough for the habit to take hold. Then, your brain will take over and you will free-flow.

For this example, let's think of a task, the task of reading and how our attitude has everything to do with the release of our potential. How do you feel about reading your assignments? You will get plenty of things to read during the course of your education. When you get a reading assignment, if you like reading, you enjoy it. Your attitude is working for you. It releases your potential to read and your attitude isn't in the way. Because you like it, you keep doing what you need to do until you understand the material and complete the assignment.

However, if you have a negative attitude toward reading, your picture is very different. You don't enjoy it. You don't like it. Reading feels more like a have to, rather than a want to. Because of your negative attitude, you find yourself engaging in creative avoidance, finding all kinds of chores and other things that need to be done instead of reading. Or, if you do "force" yourself to read, you don't get much out of it. It isn't because you aren't capable, but more likely you are wrestling with your negative attitude.

So, how often do you read every day? How many emails, text messages, tweets, Instagrams, websites, and any other electronic communication, magazines, newspapers, etc. might you read during your day? You probably read thousands, if not tens of thousands, of words every day. What releases your potential to read them? Your attitude. Once you are capable of reading, then it is your attitude that has everything to do with the release of that potential.

When we stay focused on our goals, and we keep in front of us the reasons why we intend to do something, it is easy to influence our attitude. If not, we are stuck with the one we have and it may not be taking us in the direction that we intend.

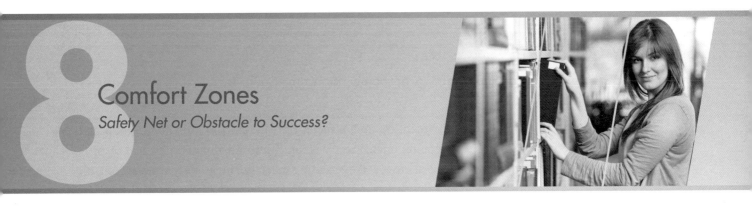

8 Comfort Zones
Safety Net or Obstacle to Success?

OVERVIEW

In our past, when we really didn't want to go somewhere or do something, we found excellent reasons for not going or doing. Dozens of them, in fact! What we may not have realized is that we were coming face-to-face with our comfort zones. While some comfort zones are good for us, others hold us back; and it is time that we learn how to expand those limiting comfort zones and allow ourselves to grow.

OBJECTIVES

By the end of this unit, I will understand:

- how I have created my current comfort zones.

- some comfort zones can keep me safe and others can keep me from growing.

- which of my current comfort zones are holding me back from expanding my life, my education and my possibilities for the future.

As human beings, we seek the familiar.

Lou Tice

KEY CONCEPTS

Anxiety: An unpleasant emotional state of apprehension, dread, or distress that exists oftentimes with no objective.

Comfort Zone: A limited area of perception and association wherein the individual/group can function effectively without experiencing uneasiness or fear; a limited, defined physical or psychological area in which a person feels at ease; self-regulating mechanism; anxiety arousal control.

Self-Regulation: Adhering to and following an internal standard.

Tension: An emotional state characterized by restlessness and anxiety; a mental state where one is thwarted from achieving an end.

NOTES

Write down your ideas, observations and insights as you work through this unit. Date your entries.

REFLECTIVE QUESTIONS

1. What do I intend my comfort zone to be when I think about getting my education? My new career?

2. In what areas might I need to stretch my comfort zone to get the grades I want?

3. What are my physical signs that I am out of my comfort zone?

4. What "soft skill" or emotional intelligence (EQ) areas might I need to stretch to get the career I want? (Example: Accountability, patience, attitude, etc.)

EXERCISE: Change Five Things

DIRECTIONS FOR IN-CLASS STUDENTS:

This is a test to see how observant you are. Pair up with another student, place your chairs back-to-back, and sit down. When the classroom is ready, you will be instructed to stand, turn to face each other, and study your partner. When instructed, sit down. Then, quickly change five (5) things about your appearance.

When instructed, stand and face your partner. Count how many of the five changed things each of you gets and enter that number here _____.

You will be instructed when to sit down, and given any further directions for this exercise.

DIRECTIONS FOR ONLINE STUDENTS:

This is a test to see how observant you are. In order to do this exercise, you will need a friend or family member to work with you. When you are both together, sit back-to-back and each of you change five (5) things about your appearance. Give yourselves about 20 seconds to do this.

When you are both finished, turn and face each other and count how many of the five changed things each of you finds. Enter that number here _____.

ALL STUDENTS

When you have completed the exercise, turn the page and review the "Responses to Change" list.

EXERCISE: Change Five Things – Responses to Change

At the conclusion of this exercise, most participants change most, if not all, of the five things back within minutes of completing the exercise. (Please keep in mind that we are talking about changing back only those items that are not necessities. If you chose to take off glasses, for example, putting them back on is a necessity!)

Why do you think most participants switch back the five things, even when they are not instructed to do so?

How would you feel if you had to go the rest of the day without changing back?

Could you do it?

Online students: When the exercise is finished, without saying anything to your partner, observe how long it takes for them to change everything back to "normal" for them. Then ask them how the exercise made them feel.

Check all that apply to you:

❑   People feel awkward and ill at ease.

❑   People think not of what they have to gain, but rather, what they have to lose.

❑   People will feel alone, even if all others around them are going through the same change.

❑   People can handle only so much change.

❑   People are at different levels of readiness to change.

❑   People are concerned they don't have enough resources.

❑   If you take the pressure off, people will revert right back to where they were.

EXERCISE: Comfort Zone Shuffle

Directions: For each situation listed in the left column, decide which zone it fits for you: the Panic Zone (No way, no how. Can't pay me enough. I choose never to do that!); the Growth Zone (I'm not comfortable now, but I could grow into it.); or the Comfort Zone (Easy, no problem. Bring it on!).

SITUATIONS	PANIC ZONE	GROWTH ZONE	COMFORT ZONE
Starting school		✓	
Going to a job interview			✓
First day at work		✓	
Sky Diving	✓		
Eating out alone			✓
Making the Honor's or Dean's list		✓	
Becoming a Tutor			✓
Letting someone read your text messages	✓		
Moving to a new town		✓	
Becoming a Supervisor		✓	✓
Becoming a Manager		✓	✓
Speaking in front of a group of peers			✓
Speaking in front of a group of strangers		✓	
Driving an expensive car			✓

Are there scenarios you have placed in the Panic Zone column that you may need to move to the Growth Zone, in order to reach your education goals? Which ones?

What insights from the Comfort Zone column might help you move some scenarios from the Panic or Growth zones?

For your Comfort Zone items, what did you do that made them comfortable for you?

Who helped you?

Where did you find your inspiration, or motivation, to keep going?

What plan or strategy (things you could actually do) will help you move some of the scenarios from Panic or Growth to Comfort?

EXERCISE: Three to Grow On

In the chart below are listed the top competencies and characteristics from the National Association of Colleges and Employers. Next to each competency, rate your current belief about yourself on a scale of 1 (lowest) to 10 (highest). Then, pick three (3) competencies that you intend to grow over the next year. Place an "X" in the column next to each.

NACE COMPETENCIES	MY RATING 1-10	PICK 3 TO GROW THIS YEAR
Communication Skills	6	
Honesty and Integrity	8	
Teamwork	8	
Interpersonal Skills	7	X
Motivation/Initiative	7	
Strong Work Ethic	8	
Flexibility/Adaptability	6	
Computer Skills	6	X
Self Confidence	4	X
Problem Solving Skills	6	
Technical Skills	5	X
Analytical Skills	8	

Of your three, what would it look like/feel like/be like if you were performing at a whole new level of effectiveness with regard to that competency or attribute?   *Visualize*

EXERCISE: Interview

Imagine you are going for a job interview; the type of job is your choice. You will be meeting with the department head or manager, someone you have never met before. Your interview time is 9:00 am, one week from today.

On your own, think about this scenario. Using your "Going For An Interview" Worksheet answers below, visualize the interview. See yourself giving the interview of a lifetime and getting the job.

GOING FOR AN INTERVIEW WORK SHEET

Where am I going to be interviewed?

How am I going to get there?

What time will I need to get out of bed?

How should I be dressed?

Who do I need to take me there?

What questions am I likely to be asked?

What questions do I want to ask?

What qualities is the interviewer probably looking for?

What sort of attitude should I have at the interview?

What is the best possible outcome for me?

If I am successful, what do I see as my next step?

SUMMARY: Fundamentals

We all know how we feel when we are "in the zone." It's "flow and go" time, because we are operating in a space where we know who we are, what we can do, and we can feel confident. Life's good, and why would we want to change that?

Let's take a minute to talk about comfort zones, what they are and what they do. Our comfort zones are defined by our habits and attitudes and our beliefs about who we are – in other words, our self-image. We can act a little better than we think we are, and a little bit worse, but as long as we are acting close to our self-image, we are in our Comfort Zone.

A good example of a comfort zone is a thermostat on a wall. We set the thermostat at 68 degrees, and if the temperature falls below to say, 66, then the furnace kicks in. If the temperature goes up to 70, then the air conditioning turns on. The key is the 68, which is the center of the thermostat's comfort zone. It could be held to a constant 68 degrees, but that would not be energy efficient, so HVAC people leave a comfort zone of about 4 degrees. We do the same in our minds, with our self-image.

The challenge comes when our comfort zones are keeping us from growing by not allowing us to be more and do more. If our comfort zones are too small, we are likely feeling frustrated by what seems like our inability to change, and yet we let our fear of growing and changing hold us back to what has always been normal for us. We let our lack of confidence or low self-efficacy build prisons of our own making.

Now when we try to grow bigger than our comfort zones, it causes tremendous tension in our system. Like the rubber band. If my lower hand is Current Reality for me, and I try to grow into something different – my upper hand – then the rubber band gets taut, and so do I. Like the tension in the rubber band, I get tense and anxious, and all I want to do is go back where I belong.

You know how this feels, if you get called up to give a speech or presentation in front of a group of people – one of your least comfortable situations. You get all sweaty, your memory goes blank, your heart starts pounding and you start to hyperventilate and your knees start to give out. And what is your self-talk saying? "GET ME OUTTA HERE!!!!" So much for trying to grow beyond your comfort zone, right? Wrong. There is a way.

As I mentioned before, your comfort zones – and we all have a lot of different comfort zones within us – are defined by our self-image. And what defines our self-image? That picture we hold of ourselves, in our subconscious. So, in order to change our self-image, we need to create new, replacement pictures. And how do we do that? By monitoring our self-talk, and changing the words we use that are creating those small comfort zones.

It's a matter of taking your imagination into the future. You practice in your mind with people that normally make you upset. You take yourself into the way your life is going to be in the future. You practice taking yourself and familiarizing yourself with where you want the job and who you want to be with. You allow yourself to travel there, safely, over and over and over.

You're going to see later on that if I can't visualize the future with safety, I won't do it. I won't do it, or I'll just do it once. Then, back I go. But I won't admit to myself the truth. I'll just say to myself, "It was stupid." "I didn't like it." "It rained too much." You will find reasons to go back.

Watch yourself in your comfort zones. School could have been out of your comfort zone, but you are here now. Universities could be out of your comfort zone. They "used to be" out of your comfort zone, right? Going into business for yourself could be out of your comfort zone.

Now, you could be very comfortable in school, but when you go to get a job, you're out of your comfort zone in the interview. Take yourself, in your imagination, and get comfortable with the future you want.

Comfort zones are not a bad thing. Some comfort zones keep us safe, and keep us from doing some pretty stupid things – like running across the freeway with cars whizzing by at 60 miles per hour, or walking alone through a dangerous part of town. It's the comfort zones that are holding us back that we want to change, if we truly want to be more than we are today.

We want to bite off more than we can chew, and then grow into the person who can take an even bigger bite! And while we are growing ourselves, we are also growing those around us – our families and friends – because we are living examples of what is possible for them, too.

SUMMARY: Application

Let me ask you, what would you think of a parent, grandparent, guardian, or caregiver of any kind if the very first day they introduced the idea of pre-school or kindergarten to a child was the first day they pulled up in front of the building and said, "Get out, I'll see you at 4:30." If you did manage to get the child out of the car, the child would be attached to the bumper as you tried to pull away.

The panic in the child would have little or nothing to do with aspects of attending school but rather everything to do with the fact that the child is being introduced to school with having no idea what school is. The child's comfort zone would be completely shattered. There was no introduction to the "new normal" that school would bring. It almost sounds nonsensical that anyone would do this to a child. But how often do we do it to ourselves?

We throw ourselves into situations without ever taking the time to prepare our mind for what is to come before we are actually in the situation. So let's go back to that child. What might you do far before the first day of preschool or kindergarten actually begins? You talk about school, you play school, you talk about all the wonderful things the child is going to learn, all the friends they are going to make, etc. You may start doing this with the child years before the first day of school actually begins. You are simply changing the construct in the child's mind. The more vivid the picture the more excited the child becomes. The child is creating the new normal of what school will look like, feel like, be like far before she is ever actually there.

So what happens when the first day school actually begins? The child can't wait. They have one foot out of the car before you even stop it and run to the door without even saying goodbye. But what about the person dropping the child off? Tears. We spent all the time preparing the child for the new normal and no time preparing ourselves. You can't just do it for others, or wait for others to do it for you. You need to do it for yourself. It is essential to grow your own mind into the new normal far before you are actually there.

9 Setting Benchmarks for My Future
What Do I Want?

OVERVIEW

So far, we have learned about how we think, and about all the things that get in the way of us being all that we can be. Now it is time to start looking at those things about ourselves and our lives that we want to change – those goals we want to set for the futures we want: a good education, graduation, job and career – to live a life closer to our true potential.

OBJECTIVES

By the end of this unit, I will understand:

- how to create a goal.

- the importance of my imagination and power of visualization in creating replacement pictures of what I want (my goals).

- that my goals throw my system out of order, so that energy and ideas are created to move me in the direction of my strongest picture.

*Human beings are always working
for order in their minds.*

LouTice

KEY CONCEPTS

Creative Subconscious: The source of mental processes that leads to solutions, ideas, conceptualizations, artistic forms, theories, or products that are unique and novel.

Goal(s): A sought end that may be actual and objective, or internal, subjective and operational; conceived future; distal goals are end-results, targets; proximal goals are near-term means to the end-result.

Goal-Setting: The act of establishing what we want.

Goal-Set Through: Goal-setting beyond current goals, in order to keep higher levels of energy and creativity active.

NOTES

Write down your ideas, observations and insights as you work through this unit. Date your entries.

....

....

....

....

....

....

....

....

....

....

....

....

....

....

....

....

....

....

....

....

REFLECTIVE QUESTIONS

1. List five (5) short-term (next few weeks) goals:

2. List three (5) long-term (six months or longer) goals:

3. From my answers to questions 1 and 2 above, have I been thinking about these goals for a long time, or just now in order to answer the questions? Why?

4. What is it going to take from me to reach these goals?

EXERCISE: My Mini-Bucket List

Part 1: Below, list 10 things you want – goals, aspirations, accomplishments, experiences – that you'd like to have or do before you die.

DESCRIBE WHAT YOU WANT	EFFICACY APPRAISAL
1.	
2.	
3.	
4.	
5.	
6.	
7.	
8.	
9.	
10.	

Part 2: Now go back, and for each item, provide your efficacy appraisal, on a scale of 1 (lowest efficacy) to 5 (highest efficacy) on your ability to achieve each goal.

If you appraise your efficacy at a 5, it means that in your mind, this goal is a "done deal." Nothing is going to stop you from accomplishing it.

If you appraise your efficacy at a 1, it means that you really can't see yourself accomplishing it and, in fact, can't believe you actually wrote it down!

Scores between 2 and 4 really depend upon how clear, confident and assured you are at accomplishing the goal.

EXERCISE: Balance Wheel Drill Down

Take a look at your Balance Wheel areas from Unit 4, page 50, and focus down a little further on what is important to you for your life.

BALANCE WHEEL AREAS	WHAT DOES IT PRESENTLY LOOK LIKE, FEEL LIKE?	WHAT DO I WANT IT TO LOOK LIKE?

EXERCISE: Situation Drill Down

Take a look at these situations regarding school and your future career and focus down a little further on what you really want it to look like.

SITUATION	WHAT DOES IT PRESENTLY LOOK LIKE, FEEL LIKE?	WHAT DO I WANT IT TO LOOK LIKE?
Attending or logging into class daily		
Taking tests		
Giving a presentation		
Answering questions in front of others		
Interviewing for a job		
Writing clearly		
Being assertive		
Accomplishing tasks with a team		
Getting along with a difficult classmate		

EXERCISE: Bad Stress vs. Good Stress – Part 1

Stress: *Def.* a physical, chemical, or emotional factor that causes bodily or mental tension and may be a factor in disease causation; a state resulting from a stress; *especially:* one of bodily or mental tension resulting from factors that tend to alter an existent equilibrium <job-related *stress*>

Eustress: *Def.* The word *eustress* consists of two parts. The prefix *eu-* derives from the Greek word meaning either "well" or "good." When attached to the word *stress,* it literally means "good stress." Eustress is not defined by the stressor type, but rather how one perceives that stressor (in other words, a negative threat versus a positive challenge). Eustress refers to a positive response one has to a stressor, which can depend on one's current feelings of control, desirability, location, and timing of the stressor.

DIRECTIONS: In the middle column, list your course schedule. Then, based on the definitions above, check the proper column for Stress or Eutress for each course.

STRESS	COURSE SCHEDULE	EUSTRESS

• What can I change about my attitudes to move the Stress courses toward Eustress?

EXERCISE: Bad Stress vs. Good Stress – Part 2

DIRECTIONS: In the middle column below, list the areas from your Balance Wheel. When you think about your balance wheel and the areas where you would like to grow, which ones cause you Stress or Eustress? Check the appropriate columns.

STRESS	BALANCE WHEEL AREAS	EUSTRESS

- If I have labeled some Balance Wheel areas as Stress, why do I feel that way?

- What can I do to change the attitudes?

SUMMARY: Fundamentals

What is a goal? Very simply, a goal is something you want. If I ask you, "What do you want?" your answers are your goals. You may want a college degree. You may want a better job, with higher earning potential. You may want to be able to buy a house or a car. Maybe you want an A on your next math test. It really doesn't matter what it is that you want. Your wants become your goals.

Some goals, like getting an A on an upcoming test, are short-term goals. If the test is next week, then that's pretty short-term. However, the goal of being able to buy a house may take a while to achieve, so that would be a long-term goal. Watching your grandchildren graduate from college would be an even longer, long-term goal. The one thing they all have in common is an end, something that lets us know that we have achieved the goal. How we get to those ends can be straightforward, or the path may twist and turn along the way.

There is another thing that our wants have in common: for every want, there is a picture of it we are holding in our minds. How clear, how vivid, that picture is determines how strong the picture is. And, we have already learned that we move toward the strongest picture we hold in our Subconscious. If we want it badly enough, we can see it, hear it, taste it, feel it – it is almost as if the goal is real. And the more real that picture is in our minds, the better the chance we will figure out a way to achieve that goal.

Remember way back, toward the beginning of this course, we talked about the functions of the Creative Subconscious. It maintains our reality, our current picture of who we believe we are. Another function of the Creative Subconscious is to solve or resolve problems. When the Creative Subconscious perceives a gap between the reality it is supposed to be maintaining internally and the world outside, it provides energy and creativity to get back to what is "normal" for us. Or rather, it provides energy and creativity to move us to the strongest picture. Backward or forward, it doesn't care. It just wants to maintain reality. Keep this in mind, because when we set new goals, we are creating that gap, and in order to move to the new reality, we need to make the replacement picture stronger than our old one.

The other thing the Creative Subconscious does, when it perceives a gap – which is also known as cognitive dissonance – is it opens up our awareness, working with the energy and creativity, to move us to the new picture, the new goal. Remember the RAS? Setting a new goal, causing that gap, has the Creative Subconscious opening up our Reticular Activating System to go after the knowledge we need to achieve the goal.

And this is all a part of who we are already. We are simply employing the tools we have in our minds, and going after the things that we want – our new goals.

When you're out of order, you are at your creative best. When you set a goal, you invent how to achieve it. When you set a goal, you come up with ideas on how to get it done. You don't need to know any ideas of how you're going to do something before you set the goal. You set the goal and your Subconscious gives you the ideas on how to do it.

Some people will set their goal only as big as they know how to accomplish it. "Do you know how to do it?" "No, I don't know." "Well then, back it up to what you do know." No, set the goal based upon what you want, and your Subconscious will create a way. If you don't have enough knowledge inside you, your

Subconscious will have you read a book. It will have you meet people, have you study. What you're doing is creating, inside yourself, the thirst for knowledge. "I've gotta have it, gotta have it." I've given myself this problem.

When you're out of order, it's natural inside of a human being to create order. Your job will be to throw your system out of order by visualizing yourself already achieving the goal, being the person you want, having the income you want, having the business that you want, having the family, having the home, having the apartment, whatever it is you want. You will see it as though you actually have it.

Your job is to create dissatisfaction in yourself, which is self-motivation. Create dissatisfaction in yourself by visualizing yourself already having graduated, already having the career, already having the job, already having the business. "I've won the game." "I have the business." "I have graduated." "I have the income." Your Subconscious looks around and says, "You don't have it. You have a problem." You are supposed to have problems.

Make yourself out of order, and unleash the creativity you have inside of you to get you what you want.

There is one very interesting thing about goals and the way that we think. Remember we are picture-oriented, we are goal-oriented. If we don't have any new goals, our Creative Subconscious only releases enough energy and creativity to maintain the status quo. No new goals, no new energy. No new goals, no new ideas. Just enough is released to keep today like yesterday, and tomorrow like today.

If we are tired of the same-old, same-old, then we need to challenge ourselves with new goals. Now, when we set new goals, we also create stress in our inner system with the gap between how we always have been and how we want to be. Like the rubber band from before, we can get tense. There are two types of stress. One, distress, is negative and is caused by fear. Fear drives us away from our goals, and makes the old picture of who we are more dominant. The other kind of stress, eustress, is positive and reflects our passion for the goals we set. Our passion for what we want will help make the replacement picture more dominant, and we will fly to our goals.

One more thing about goals. As we approach achieving our goals, our drive, energy and creativity start to fade. The gap between what was and what we want has shrunk, so the Creative Subconscious is releasing less and less, the closer we get to the goal. In order to maintain our energy and ideas, we want to goal-set through our goals, to the next goal on our path. It's like always keeping the horizon beyond the current horizon in view. Now it's OK to not set another goal, but let's do it by intent – because we want to – and not by neglect, because we forgot to.

SUMMARY: Application

It was the 2nd grade. My teacher talked to us about doing the MS Read-a-Thon. It's a great cause, to raise money for MS research. So she explained how it works. Read books, sign up sponsors, and collect cash. In 2nd grade, it's not hard to get 2nd graders excited about most anything.

But then she said, by the way, the grand prize is a Gateway Clipper boat ride (which is the boat fleet that that runs on the rivers of downtown Pittsburgh, PA) with Franco Harris, running back, Pittsburgh Steelers. I was a young boy, sports fanatic, growing up in W PA, just outside of Pittsburgh. And since I was being raised in the Pittsburgh area by other sports fanatics, I had already fully assimilated from the people raising me, as most young people in our area, that my favorite NFL football team was the Pittsburgh Steelers. And it just so happened that my boyhood idol was Franco Harris.

I instantly went from goal-setting to goal-assimilating. Other children may have set the goal to meet Franco, I saw myself meeting Franco and I already knew the football he was going to sign for me. So I went to work driven by the vision, the image of meeting Franco. Now, I couldn't quit my day job, I still had to be a 2nd grader and the responsibilities of doing that.

This was the mid-1970's, a world without internet, emails, cell phones, text messages, and social media sites. The world was so much smaller in those days, especially for a young kid whose only mode of transportation was walking or my bike. So every day, I went door to door, house to house, on my bike, further and further signing up sponsors, explaining to them what I was doing and why they had to sponsor me. When the street lights came on, back to the house, reading every book I could put my fingers on. This process went on for weeks. Every night, on weekends, signing up sponsors, reading books, then back to everyone to collect the money, over and over and over again.

The end result? I read hundreds of books, signed up hundreds of sponsors, and raised far more money than any 8 year old should have been capable of raising. In fact, I raised more money than the rest of my classmates combined.

When you make the jump from goal-setting to goal-assimilating, it releases all the potential you have inside of you, but it doesn't guarantee the outcome. Just because I released every bit of energy, motivation, desire, and creativity to spend countless hours reading, traveling out to sign up sponsors, then traveling back to collect the money, over and over, it didn't guarantee the outcome I intended — meeting Franco Harris. But it was the vividness, that clear-as-the-day picture of that moment that I would shake his hand, give my football and ask him to sign it that drove me.

I will never forget the day the letter arrived in the mail. I vividly recall my mother's reaction, her excitement and amazement: truly shock, that I was going to meet Franco Harris. But also, to this day, I vividly recall my reaction. My mother was shocked. I wasn't. It is what I expected all along. Assimilating the goal didn't guarantee the outcome, but it did release all the potential I had.

I want you to think of a time in your life when you wanted something so badly you could practically taste it. It completely dominated your thoughts day and night. You had the feeling that you would do anything to have, be, change or do that which you had made up your mind you wanted. This is an example and hopefully you have many examples from your own life when you didn't just set a goal, but you assimilated it. And I'll bet in most of those instances, you also accomplished it.

Imagine if you applied even half that energy and commitment into getting your education or the career you want? Touchdown!

From My Toolbox: Change Made Easy
It's All About Replacement Pictures!

OVERVIEW

Remember that our self-talk is made up of three things: Words, which trigger Pictures, which bring on Emotion. And, we have just set some Goals for what we want in the future. Now we are going to use our Self-Talk and the Goals we set, to create powerful Affirmations that will help us achieve our goals. You see, Affirmations are the tools we use to bring about the changes that we want.

OBJECTIVES

By the end of this unit, I will understand:

- that affirmations are simply my goals put into a format that creates replacement pictures in my mind.

- the 11 guidelines for writing effective affirmations.

- how effectively written affirmations can create a magnetic draw to the future I want.

*Affirmations are simply your self-talk,
about your desired future, written down.
We want to write them down,
because our future is too important to be left to chance.*

LouTice

KEY CONCEPTS

Affirm/Affirmation/Affirmation Process: A statement of fact; an internal, cognitive act that establishes a specific course, direction, outcome, or state of being for the future; a confirmation or ratification of a truth.

Self-Talk: An act whereby one evaluates or assesses one's behavior; how one talks or reaffirms to oneself when one reacts to one's own evaluation, or others' evaluations of one's performance. Self-talk may have an affirming influence in establishing self-image.

NOTES

Write down your ideas, observations and insights as you work through this unit. Date your entries.

....

....

....

....

....

....

....

....

....

....

....

....

....

....

....

....

....

....

....

....

REFLECTIVE QUESTIONS

1. Is it necessary to write down goals or is it OK to keep them in your head? Why?

2. What attributes do I see in others, who have the career that I intend to have for myself, attributes that I would like to emulate?

3. In what areas of my life might I be dodging accountability?

SUMMARY: Fundamentals

We have talked about how our thoughts accumulate to become our beliefs, and our thoughts are created by the words we use, that trigger pictures, and then we attach emotions or feelings to those pictures. These thoughts are commonly called our self-talk. We have used our self-talk in the past to create and reinforce the self-image that we hold of ourselves, saved in our subconscious mind.

We have learned that it is possible to change those old pictures that are holding us back from achieving all that we want for our futures. And it will be the strength of those replacement pictures we create that will move us forward.

We are now going to learn a formalized process for harnessing our self-talk, in the most efficient and effective way possible, to move us toward our goals quickly and painlessly. We are going to take our goals, those things we want, and write them into a format known as Affirmations. There are 11 simple guidelines to writing effective affirmations that will help you to free-flow your behavior without needing to consciously think about it. And it's all about creating those replacement pictures that drive the changes we want.

Here's the kind of imagery that changes that inside you. It is experiential imagery. It is first person imagery. It is present tense imagery. It is positive imagery. I keep seeing the end results and assimilating the end results into me, letting my subconscious create the "how."

Keep in mind that affirmations are not an end result. The affirmations are a means to get you the end result. The affirmation process is to change the construct in your brain, because once you've decided the change you want, writing it out is very important.

Every affirmation will be only one sentence long. Not a paragraph. It needs to be one sentence.

When you write them out, it's **Personal.** If somebody else was to read them, it would sound selfish. I can't affirm for you. I can only affirm for me. You will sound like "I am" or "I have" or "it's easy for me." It is Personal.

The second step is **Positive.** I want to create the picture I'm moving toward. I want to create an idea for my mind that causes me to seek it.

Present Tense. Simply, it means all of your goals are written as though you already are where you want to be. You already have what it is you're seeking. It's the future in the present tense.

Achievement. Sometimes people say, "I can be a good person." I can or I will. "I can be nice, I'm just not." "I can" is only speaking of your potential, not of the result. Do you see the difference? You're speaking that the potential is inside when you say, "I can." But to say "I have, I am, it is" and look around and it's not, wow, you've got a problem. You are supposed to have.

No Comparisons. Comparing yourself, being better than, greater than, is not at all going to help you be successful. You want to observe others, use others as a model, take their attributes and assimilate those into yourself like you'd like to have them. You're building a better you, not someone else.

Action Words. Real life is moving pictures, not paintings on a wall. So you put in words like, "I quickly, I easily, I fluidly, I aggressively," because you want your pictures to move.

Emotion Words. The power comes in the emotion. So you put the appropriate emotion. "It makes me feel proud to be…" "It brings great joy…" "I feel enthusiastic about…" The more emotion, the faster the change.

Accuracy. "I'm going to lose some weight." Clarity, exactness, being explicit is what you need. You'll have trouble forcing yourself to be clear. Why do you suppose people would have difficulty being clear? It makes you accountable. If you can't get it clear, it's because either you haven't spent the time to focus, or you're dodging accountability.

Balance is very important. When you are starting out goal setting, it's essential. You are going to run obsessively with this process. You are going to become obsessive inside yourself. You are going to drive yourself like you've never been driven before.

Keep your goals and affirmations **Realistic.** You can't take yourself past what you can imagine yourself doing. You need to be able to fully see yourself in the new picture. And then as you start approaching your goal, you re-set and go past it.

You want to keep your affirmations **Confidential.** For a variety of reasons, confidentiality is very important. If you tell somebody you're going to do it, it becomes a have-to-goal. You force yourself into it and you work against it. You don't need to be pushed into, or forced into change.

You want to grow into it.

SUMMARY: Application

I have applied the affirmation process to my own life, deliberately since 1995. But, honestly, I was fortunate. Lou Tice, The Pacific Institute, the almost 18 years of formal education, countless hours of training, seminars, and professional development that I had amassed to that point in my life hadn't convinced me to work this process to change my life. Nikki McNew did.

I was teaching a group of students how to write their goals in sentence form, the affirmation process, when she simply asked me in front of an entire room of students: "Mr. Fitz, do you do affirmations?" I felt like I was back in that 5th grade spelling bee all over again, with all eyes on me, not knowing how to respond. You see, I wasn't. I was teaching it, but I wasn't applying it. Thank you, Nikki McNew. It isn't knowing the information that changes you. It is applying it.

This is the affirmation I started the process with in 1995. "I have a clear and defined set of goals and I review them twice a day." What was currently true of me at the time was I didn't have a clear and defined set of goals and I didn't review them. Therefore, no change necessary to change the same person I already was with regard to goal setting. So I began to work the process in my mind. "I have a clear and defined set of goals and I review them twice a day." I would read the statement, picture writing and thinking through goals in all kinds of areas in my life and then let the emotions of excitement, exhilaration, anticipation, passion well up in side of me. It was the excitement of creating my own future.

Notice my starting point. My first affirmation was an affirmation about doing affirmations. I had to see myself working the process, taking the time to identify goals and aspirations I have for my life. Before long, I actually began writing goals, then reading, picturing, and feeling. I affirm goals in all areas of my life – goals upon goals. I didn't force myself into using the affirmation process. I grew myself into it.

You may also want to start with an affirmation about doing affirmations if you are not already doing so. Then, begin to be more intentional about your education. Write affirmations about attendance, participation, grades, the skills you intend to acquire, the diploma, certification, or degree you intend to have. See the future in the present tense so vividly that you drive yourself toward it.

AFFIRMATION WORKSHOP
REFLECTION AND PREPARATION FOR WRITING AFFIRMATIONS

1. Take time to go back and review all the activities and exercises you have done, so far, that can help you identify and further clarify the goals that you want to affirm. Reviewing the following exercises might help you:

   - Meaningful Change, Unit 2

   - Maintaining Sanity, Unit 2

   - Balance Wheel, Unit 4

   - Imagination[2], Unit 4

   - Building My Self-Efficacy, Unit 6

   - Habits Inventory, Unit 7

   - Comfort Zone Shuffle, Unit 8

   - My Mini-Bucket List, Unit 9

   - Balance Wheel Drill Down, Unit 9

2. Review your Personal Balance Wheel. Are there areas you want to change, delete, add?

3. Review your personal notes for specific applications and areas you intend to include in your affirmations.

4. Reflect on what is important to you. What do you want in your life that you don't currently have? What do you want it to look like?

5. Consider the important people in your life: mother, father, siblings, children, nieces or nephews, grandparents, even friends.

   - How do your goals affect the people on your list?

   - How might your longer-term goals affect the people closest to you?

   - As you move forward, toward your goals, how might these people help you to maintain your energy, passion and commitment?

6. Go to Create Your Own Balance Wheel and complete a new Wheel, after you have considered your answers to 1 through 5 above.

7. Your facilitator will guide you through the Affirmation Workshop.

THOUGHT PATTERNS FOR A SUCCESSFUL CAREER®
Mastering the Attitude of Success™ • Participant Manual
©The Pacific Institute®, LLC

AFFIRMATION WORKSHOP

In this session, you learn how to write affirmations and practice writing them. You will use the goal ideas you have worked on. An affirmation is a statement of fact or belief. When written correctly, an affirmation will trigger a picture in your mind of your goal already accomplished. Your affirmations are your tools to deliberately control your own forethought. As you have learned, this is how successful, high-performance people win so frequently. You can paint your own positive scenarios, change your picture on the inside first, and automatically gravitate toward your goals by using these tools. There are 11 basic guidelines for writing affirmations. Review them closely.

1. **Personal:** Affirmations are written with the word "I" in them. You can only affirm for yourself. The desired change will come about because of something you do, and it is your own inner picture that will change because of your affirmation.

2. **Positive:** Always describe what you want in your affirmation. Describe what you want to move toward, not what you want to move away from. What would it look like if it were fixed?

3. **Present Tense:** Affirmations are written as though they are happening right now. This requires using your imagination and becomes easier with practice.

4. **Indicate Achievement:** Eliminate words such as, "can, will, should, and want to" etc., from your affirmations. Include phrases such as, "I am, I do," or "I have." It is important to give your subconscious a clear picture of the end result as though it is already accomplished.

5. **No Comparisons:** Comparing yourself to others is ineffective. The technique of affirming is a personal process. Your measurement of growth is based on yourself.

6. **Action Words:** Use terms that describe and trigger action pictures, such as "easily, quickly, thrive on, energetically, confidently," in your affirmations.

7. **Emotion Words:** These are of critical importance. The more positive emotion you feel when picturing your accomplished goal, the faster your affirmation will work for you.

8. **Accuracy:** If your goal is to exercise regularly, what kind of exercise? Is it jogging, walking, swimming, aerobics, or something else? How regularly? Three times a week? If so, on what days? What time of day and for how long? This is how accurate your affirmations must be. If written in general terms, the picture is too vague and it gives you too many escape routes.

9. **Balance:** Set goals and write affirmations in all areas of your life.

10. **Realistic:** After you have written your affirmation, close your eyes and picture it. Can you see yourself there? You need to be able to see it, visualize it, and imagine it.

11. **Confidential:** Share your affirmations with only those you are certain will support and help you achieve them. Most of your personal affirmations need not be shared.

CREATE YOUR OWN BALANCE WHEEL

On the Balance Wheel, list the areas of your life you would like to improve or change. For example: career, spiritual, family, physical and mental health, education, financial, etc. Refer to the ideas you have written in previous units, particularly Unit 4, page 90.

On page 169, write an affirmation for each area listed on your Balance Wheel using the process of Vision, Current Reality, Affirmation. Refer to the Affirmation Checklist on page 171, and the Action/Emotion Words on pages 165-167. When you have completed this, transfer them to 3x5 cards or your Affirmation Assistant app.

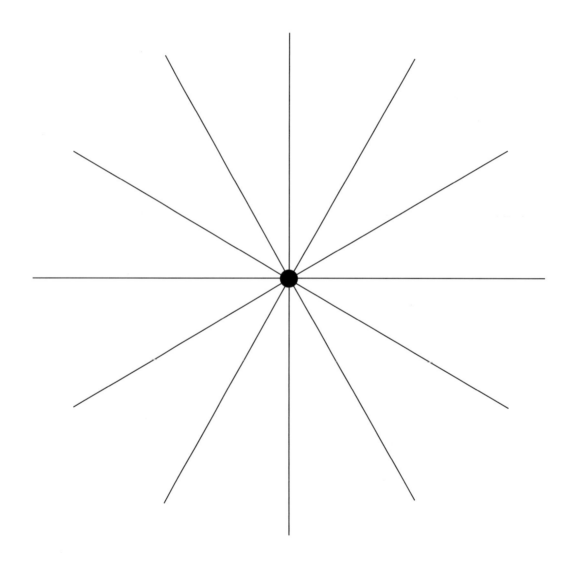

• Personal	• Family	• Health/Physical	• Health/Mental
• Spiritual	• Social	• Career/Vocation/Job	• Retirement
• Marriage	• Educational	• Recreational/Leisure Time	• Community Services

MINI BALANCE WHEELS

For further clarification of your balance wheel areas or goal areas, it helps to take each area and break it down into its component parts. Take a general area from your Balance Wheel (from page 90 or 162 and drill it down to more specific goals within the larger Goal. (For help, go to your Balance Wheel Drill Down exercise on page 146.)

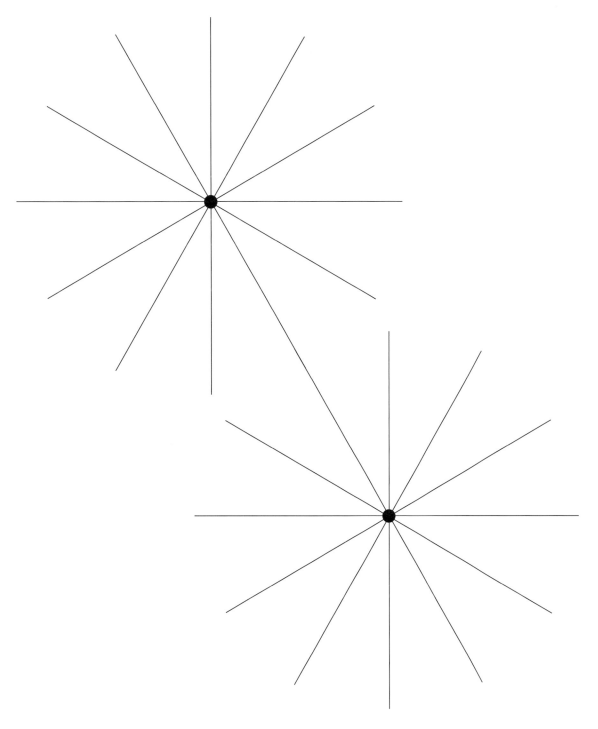

SAMPLE AFFIRMATIONS

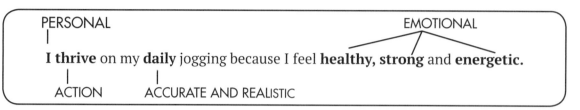

The following list has a variety of sample affirmations that may be helpful. Some may fit your career situation, others focus on your personal life, and some may overlap. If some of these affirmations work for you, please use them, but be sure to rewrite them so that they are you talking to you.

EDUCATION SPECIFIC SAMPLES

1. I have an excellent, free-flowing memory with clear and easy recall.

2. I have a positive expectancy of earning good grades, and I see all setbacks as temporary.

3. I have pride in my educational performance and positive expectations of my future.

4. I am accountable for the results of my decisions and actions.

5. I speak clearly and calmly and make positive contributions that benefit me and my peers.

6. Taking tests is easy for me because I study and prepare for them well in advance.

7. I am calm, relaxed and clear-headed when I ask questions in class.

8. Giving presentations in front of my classmates is fun and uplifting.

9. Because I am well organized and plan ahead, I have reliable transportation to school and back.

CAREER SAMPLES

1. I enthusiastically arrive at work on time and attend meetings with an open mind and a positive attitude.

2. I am very effective and efficient, especially in stressful situations.

3. I develop feelings of respect and self-esteem in myself and others.

4. Because I sincerely care about myself and the quality of my life, I am financially responsible.

5. My family and friends are benefiting from the successes that have come from my hard work.

6. I reinforce my successes and positively correct for errors.

7. I am a successful professional and earn $_____ per month. I live a comfortable and happy life.

8. Because I am well organized, I enjoy my neat and orderly office.

PERSONAL ATTRIBUTES SAMPLES

1. I like and respect myself, because I know that I am a worthy, capable and valuable person.

2. I enjoy my life and my relationships with other people.

3. It is easy and fun to write and imprint affirmations daily.

4. I enjoy making positive affirmations daily, because of the positive and quick results I get.

5. I quietly do helpful and worthwhile things for others.

6. I look for ways of uplifting myself and others, and I do it with ease every day.

7. I am my own expert, and I accept only positive attitudes and opinions from others.

8. Because of the warmth and love I show my children, I teach them to show warmth and love to each other.

9. I am healthy and energetic, because I treat my body with the love and respect I deserve.

ACTION/EMOTION WORDS Circle 15-20 words that speak to you.

Accepted	Comfortable	Effortless	Fulfilling
Accomplish	Comic	Electric	Fun
Achieve	Compassionate	Elegant	Gallant
Acknowledge	Competent	Eloquent	Generous
Active	Complete	Embrace	Genial
Adaptable	Complimentary	Encouraging	Gentle
Admire	Composed	Endearing	Genuine
Adorable	Concise	Enduring	Gifted
Adventurous	Confident	Energetic	Giving
Affectionate	Conscientious	Enjoyable	Glad
Agreeable	Considerate	Enlightened	Glorious
Aggressive	Constructive	Enterprising	Good
Alert	Content	Entertaining	Graceful
Amazing	Cooperative	Enthused	Gracious
Ambitious	Courteous	Enthusiastic	Grammatical
Articulate	Creative	Excellent	Grand
Aspiring	Cultured	Exceptional	Great
Assertive	Curious	Exciting	Growing
Assured	Dazzling	Expectant	Handy
Attentive	Decisive	Expressive	Happy
Beautiful	Delightful	Faithful	Harmonious
Beloved	Dependable	Famous	Healthy
Blessed	Deserving	Fantastic	Hearty
Blissful	Determined	Fascinating	Helpful
Brave	Devote	Fearless	Honest
Bright	Dignified	Feminine	Honorable
Brilliant	Diligent	Fervent	Hospitable
Calm	Diplomatic	Festive	Humble
Capable	Disciplined	Flexible	Humorous
Caring	Dramatic	Fluent	Idealistic
Charming	Dutiful	Forceful	Illustrious
Cheerful	Dynamic	Forgiving	Immense
Clean	Eager	Fortunate	Impartial
Clear	Easy	Fresh	Impeccable
Clever	Effective	Friendly	Important
Colorful	Efficient	Frugal	Impressive

ACTION/EMOTION WORDS

Independent	Mellow	Principled	Safe
Individualistic	Melodious	Privileged	Scholarly
Industrious	Memorable	Productive	Secure
Influential	Merry	Professional	Seeing
Ingenious	Mighty	Proficient	Seeking
Innovative	Modest	Progressive	Selective
Inspiring	Moral	Promising	Self-confident
Inspirational	Motivated	Prosperous	Self-contained
Instrumental	Musical	Proud	Self-reliant
Intellectual	Myself	Prudent	Sensational
Intelligent	Natural	Punctual	Sensible
Intense	Neighborly	Pure	Sensitive
Intentional	Noble	Purposeful	Sentimental
Intuitive	Nourishing	Qualified	Serene
Inventive	Obedient	Quick	Sharing
Jolly	Obliging	Quiet	Significant
Jovial	Outstanding	Quotable	Simply
Joyous	Passionate	Radiant	Sincere
Jubilant	Patient	Rapid	Skillful
Just	Patriotic	Rational	Smiling
Kind	Peaceful	Realistic	Smart
Knowing	Perceptive	Reasonable	Smooth
Knowledgeable	Persevering	Receptive	Sociable
Learned	Personable	Refined	Sophisticated
Likeable	Placid	Refreshing	Sparkling
Lively	Pleasant	Regal	Special
Lovable	Pleasing	Relaxed	Spectacular
Lovely	Pleasurable	Reliable	Speedy
Loving	Polite	Reputable	Spirited
Loyal	Positive	Resourceful	Spiritual
Lucky	Powerful	Respectable	Splendid
Luminous	Practical	Respected	Spontaneous
Lyrical	Praiseworthy	Respectful	Sporting
Magnetic	Precise	Responsible	Stable
Magnificent	Prepared	Retentive	Stalwart
Marvelous	Presentable	Reverent	Steadfast
Meaningful	Prestigious	Rich	Steady

ACTION/EMOTION WORDS

Strong	Terrific	Unforgettable	Warm
Strengthen	Thankful	Universal	Wealthy
Stylish	Thorough	Uplifting	Welcome
Stunning	Thrifty	Useful	Well
Sturdy	Thriving	Valiant	Wholesome
Successful	Timely	Valuable	Willing
Super	Tireless	Venturesome	Winner
Superb	Tolerant	Vibrant	Winning
Supportive	Tranquil	Victorious	Wonderful
Sure	Treasured	Vigorous	Working
Survivor	Thoughtful	Virtuous	Worthwhile
Swift	Triumphant	Visible	Worthy
Sympathetic	True	Visionary	Young
Systematic	Trusted	Visual	Youthful
Tactful	Trustworthy	Vital	Zealously
Teachable	Truthful	Vivacious	Zestful
Tender	Understanding	Vivid	

WORDS TO AVOID

Better	Need to
But	Never
Can	Not
Could	Should
Even if	Some
Going to	Something
Have to	Try
Hope to	Want to
Less	Will
Maybe	Wish
Might	Would
More	Would like to

GROUP EXERCISE

In groups of three or four, write an affirmation for each of the following situations as if you were the person with the challenge. Recognize that the person in current reality wants to change. The vision is what it looks like without the challenge. Refer to the checklist on page 171 and the samples on page 164.

CURRENT REALITY	VISION
Denise feels she is too old to learn anything new, but she wants to use computers.	

AFFIRMATION:

Melanie is often late for class and classmates are beginning to notice.	

AFFIRMATION:

Juanita has ongoing transportation problems she would like to be able to solve.	

AFFIRMATION:

Maurice gets so nervous before making presentations that he "blows it". He wants to do well.	

AFFIRMATION:

Kurt has been concerned about his student loan. He feels very frustrated and worried.	

AFFIRMATION:

THOUGHT PATTERNS FOR A SUCCESSFUL CAREER®
Mastering the Attitude of Success™ • Participant Manual
©The Pacific Institute®, LLC

WRITING AFFIRMATIONS

Now, individually, write three sample affirmations for yourself, following the same process with each. Refer to the list of helpful Action/Emotion Words on pages 165 through 167 and the Affirmation Checklist on page 171.

CURRENT REALITY *(to move away from)*	VISION *(to include in your affirmation)*
bad temper	calm, clear minded
lazy	energetic
procrastinate	accomplish immediately

CURRENT REALITY   VISION

AFFIRMATION:

CURRENT REALITY   VISION

AFFIRMATION:

CURRENT REALITY   VISION

AFFIRMATION:

5 COLUMN AFFIRMATION WRITING GUIDE

Current Reality Present State	Potential Loss Emotion-Feeling	Vision Desired State	Why? Personal Value Emotion-Feeling	Affirmation Personal-Positive-Clear Balance-Action-Emotion I x V = R
A statement describing the "now."	What is the "now" costing you? • Effect on you • Feeling	What does it look like without the problem?	What does that desired state "give" me?	

AFFIRMATION CHECKLIST

Take each of your affirmations and check them against the list below. Does each affirmation give you a clear, concise, vivid picture of what you want?

❑ **Personal** – Include *I* or *me*.

❑ **Positive** – Describe what you want instead of what you don't want.

❑ **Present Tense** – Write like it's happening right now.

❑ **Indicate Achievement** – Use phrases such as *I have, I am* and *I do.* Do not include terms like *can, will, want to* and *should.*

❑ **No Comparisons** – Picture your own change and growth instead of comparing yourself to someone else.

❑ **Action Words** – Create pictures of yourself performing in an easy, anxiety-free manner.

❑ **Emotion Words** – Cause you to feel exactly how you want to feel when it is achieved. Refer to pages 165-167 for Affirmation Action/Emotion Words.

❑ **Accuracy** – Specific and detailed. Are there any escape routes?

❑ **Balance** – Coordinate well with goals you have in other areas of your life.

- Family   • Recreation   • Social

- Spiritual • Education   • Business

- Health   • Relationship   • Career

- Financial • Other

❑ **Realistic** - Can you see yourself achieving it?

❑ **Confidential** - With whom do you choose to share this affirmation? Who will really support and help you to achieve it? Most of your personal affirmations need not be shared.

Seeing Myself in the Future
If I Can See It, I Can Be It

OVERVIEW

Writing our affirmations is just the beginning. Now it is time to assimilate those desired futures into our Subconscious so that we can start making those changes we want. We are going to use another "natural" tool that has always been at our disposal – our teleological nature. We seek the strongest pictures. The words of our affirmations create vibrant pictures of who and what we want to be, and we use the visualization process to make the new picture stronger than the old.

OBJECTIVES

By the end of this unit, I will understand:

- the process of visualizing my affirmations – by reading, picturing and feeling the emotions – to unleash the power and creativity of my mind.

- that the power in my affirmations is in the words I choose, to create vivid pictures and emotions.

- I can read, picture and feel my affirmations as often as I want to during each day (but not while I am driving!).

As you visualize the new, you become dissatisfied with the old.

LouTice

KEY CONCEPTS

Assimilate/Assimilation: The incorporating of an idea or thought into the subconscious; the absorption or process of incorporating something external into one's body or cognitive processes; making new visions a part of our lives; e.g., one learns and can behaviorally manifest mastery of fundamental mathematical processes.

Forethought: Thinking ahead.

Performance Reality: How one acts and performs based on one's currently dominant self-image.

Visualize (Visualization): To recall or form mental images from the imagination; to make perceptive to the mind; forethought; mental stimulation. Creative visualization is often a means of unblocking or dissolving barriers that we ourselves have created.

NOTES

Write down your ideas, observations and insights as you work through this unit. Date your entries.

REFLECTIVE QUESTIONS

1. What obstacles do I see, that might get in the way of establishing a "Read – Picture – Feel" routine, for assimilating my new affirmations?

2. Here is how I am going to work around those obstacles, giving myself and my affirmations the best chance for success:

3. Other than first thing in the morning and right before going to sleep, what other "best times" of the day could I add to my visualization routine?

EXERCISE: Lemon Visualization

CLASSROOM DIRECTIONS: One person in the class will read the following, while the rest of the class sits comfortably and quietly in their chairs, eyes closed, allowing their minds to picture the following scenario.

ONLINE DIRECTIONS: Either read the following to yourself, have a friend or family member read it to you, or you read it to the friend or family member. Whoever is doing the listening, sit comfortably and quietly, with eyes closed, and allow your mind to picture the following scenario. For the reader, note any reactions or comments from the listener when the exercise is finished.

SCENARIO:

Close your eyes and relax. Imagine yourself going into your kitchen. Now you're headed toward your refrigerator. **[Pause]**

Open the door and go into the bin where you keep the fruit. Reach in and get a lemon. **[Pause]**

Close the door and go over to your counter. Now visualize taking the lemon in your hand and rolling it back and forth until it's soft. See the color and feel the texture.

Get a knife from your cutlery drawer and slice the lemon in half. Watch the spray as the knife cuts through the skin. **[Pause]** See the juice as it spills on the counter. **[Pause]**

Now take one half of the lemon and bring it close to your mouth...closer... closer...

You can smell the freshness and feel the juiciness. **[Pause]**

Now take a big bite.

NOTES

....

....

....

....

....

....

....

EXERCISE: Affirmation Adaptation and Visualization

My family and friends are benefiting from the successes that have come from my hard work and commitment to my education.

I enthusiastically arrive at school on time and attend my classes daily with an open mind and a positive attitude.

Taking tests is easy for me because I study and prepare for them well in advance.

I have a clear and defined set of goals and I review them twice a day.

I am calm, confident, and articulate when speaking about my talents and abilities to perform in this job, because I am qualified, prepared and deserve a new career.

Choose one of the affirmations from above, and re-write it below to make it personal for you.

_____

_____

_____

_____

Now, read your revised affirmation. See the result you want. Feel the positive emotions of your successful achievement.

Did you get a vibrant picture? Was the emotion strong enough to pull you toward your new goal? If not, what words could be changed to give you a clearer picture, with stronger emotions?

_____

_____

_____

Write out your new, revised affirmation:

_____

_____

_____

_____

THOUGHT PATTERNS FOR A SUCCESSFUL CAREER®
Mastering the Attitude of Success™ • Participant Manual
©The Pacific Institute®, LLC

EXERCISE: Habit Cycle on Assimilating Affirmations

We can use our mind's ability to create the good habit of assimilating our affirmations. In the table below, use the left column to list the different times in your day when you can focus your attention on your affirmations. Then, in the middle column, describe the routine you will use to create this new assimilation habit. And finally, in the right column, what will be your reward for working through each routine?

WHEN	WHAT ROUTINE	REWARD
Example Right before going to sleep	Read-Picture-Feel each affirmation	Gives my subconscious time while I sleep to store each replacement picture.

SUMMARY: Fundamentals

Once we have written our affirmations, there is another simple process, one which we have practiced since we were small children, to help us install the replacement pictures into our subconscious. As kids, we called it "pretend." As teenagers, our parents or teachers called it "daydreaming." Right now, we are going to call it "visualization."

For each affirmation, read the words. Then, close your eyes and see the end result, the goal, you want, and feel the positive emotions of achieving your goal. Then go to your next affirmation and read, picture and feel. On to the next and read, picture and feel. Sound familiar? It is. It is your self-talk helping you create the new replacement picture.

The more clear and vivid the words, the clearer the picture and the sharper the emotions. So, you want to write your affirmations with words that really create the positive picture of the future you want.

Read, picture and feel the emotions. The best times of the day to go through your affirmations are first thing in the morning, as you wake up, and then again at night, just before you fall asleep. Our minds are more open in this alpha state of consciousness. If you want to reach a goal faster, you can go through your affirmations at any time during the day – between classes, at lunch, while you are driving: just don't close your eyes while you are driving!

I want you to think about, "How good can I be?" "How much can I do?" Do you see how you do it? It's as easy as that. The more time you spend doing this, I promise you the greater your life will go.

Before you fall asleep, tell yourself how you want to wake up. Tell yourself exactly what time you want to wake up. You'd be surprised, even in a different time frame, you do that. You wake up at the exact time, if you're in Turkey or if you're in Europe or if you're in the United States. Your subconscious is that strong. Tell yourself how you want to feel when you wake up. Tell yourself how you want your morning to go. Tell yourself how you want your afternoon to go.

Tell yourself how you want your evening to go. If you have a special date, a special party, talk to yourself about how you want it to come out. Visualize it. Don't leave it to chance. Don't walk in with your old history, unless your old history is good enough. Prepare yourself for the day. Prepare yourself for a meeting. Prepare yourself for the class. Visualize yourself into it.

Remember: Read, picture and feel the emotions. Because we are teleological, our creative subconscious will go after these new pictures with drive and life will never be the same again. The good news? We can use this process over and over and over, every time we want to change and grow. It's renewable, and we control it.

You are probably going to feel energized by your affirmations, because of the tremendous power of the positive emotions.

THOUGHT PATTERNS FOR A SUCCESSFUL CAREER®
Mastering the Attitude of Success™ • Participant Manual
©The Pacific Institute®, LLC

SUMMARY: Application

Laura Wilkinson's dream of competing in the 2000 Sydney Olympics almost came to an end months before the Olympics began. In March 2000 she hit her right foot against a wooden board that she was jumping off of to practice her dives on dry land. She fractured three metatarsal bones and would require surgery.

The next day her coach, Ken Armstrong, knocked on her door at six o'clock in the morning and told her that he did not care if her foot had been amputated, she was going to the Olympics. There was no way that Wilkinson could have the surgery and still be ready to compete in time for the Olympics, so a cast was put on and the bones were allowed to fuse and heal just as they were. This resulted in a knot of bone on the bottom of her foot that felt, she said, like walking on a rock. The cast stayed on until just weeks before the Olympic trials, but Wilkinson used visualization and other dry-land practices to stay in the best shape that she could.

As she explained, "When I broke my foot in 2000 right before the Olympics, I would go up to the 10-meter, stand there, and go through every dive in my head. Then when I got back it wasn't as if I had missed three months. I'd been thinking about it, so the dives were much easier to get back."

Laura Wilkinson was not a favorite going into the 2000 Olympics even before she broke her foot. The Chinese team had dominated the event in the previous years, winning the gold in the platform event in every Olympics since 1984. The end result? It was the first time that an American woman had won a gold medal in platform diving since 1964. [http://www.encyclopedia.com/doc/1G2-3407900624.html]

How powerful can visualization be? According to psycho-neuromuscular theory, through mental practice Laura Wilkinson was actually producing very small muscle contractions similar to those involved with her actual dives.

Dr. Steven Ungerleider, a psychologist and one of the world's leading experts on sports, performance enhancement drugs, and fair play, describes what was happening in Laura's mind as she was visualizing her dives. By deliberate visualization she was "shooting mental faxes" and other electronic impulses to her muscles and tendons, reminding them how to leap from the springboard, prepare to tuck, rotate for several spins, and then unravel the body for a perfect no-splash entry into the pool. These messages travel at lightning speed and cause the muscles to fire at appropriate sequences so they can perform the correct sporting movement. In essence, she allowed her muscles to practice, even when her body was at rest.

This theory has been tested quite frequently by simply having athletes mentally rehearse images and then measuring the electrical activity (with an electromyograph, or EMG) in their arms and legs. In one experiment, a psychologist in Colorado measured the electrical activity of a downhill ski racer while the skier sat quietly imaging the race course. The printout of the racer's leg muscle contractions and firings corresponded exactly to the terrain of the hilly and challenging ski course. If we mentally rehearse our sports often and with great intensity, we strengthen and condition the muscle firings and neuromuscular "phone lines" so that the messages get there more efficiently and with greater clarity. [(Ungerleider, Steve (1996)]

NOTES

OVERVIEW

We have all felt, at one time or another, like we were being forced into doing something against our will. We may have done it, but we rebelled every step of the way. We felt pushed and we pushed back, and it used up a lot of energy while it made us feel unhappy. What if we put life on a "want to" basis, and used all of that energy and creativity to make a happy life for ourselves and those around us?

OBJECTIVES

By the end of this unit, I will understand:

- areas in my life where I let fear hold me back.

- that motivation can be negative and restrictive, which causes me to push back.

- putting my life on a constructive, "want to" basis moves me forward beyond my present limitations.

Do what you want to do, just accept the consequences of your actions.

LouTice

KEY CONCEPTS

Accountable/Accountability: Responsible; answerable for an outcome.

Coercive Motivation: A drive based on fear and/or authority; a have-to.

Constructive Motivation: A positive and free-flowing drive on a want-to basis.

Fear: An emotional state in the presence or anticipation of a dangerous or noxious stimulus; an internal subjective experience that is often physically manifested.

Or Else: Implicit threat for failure to act according to dictates.

Push-Push Back: When one is pushed, one unconsciously pushes back.

NOTES

Write down your ideas, observations and insights as you work through this unit. Date your entries.

REFLECTIVE QUESTIONS

1. What are the "have-to's" in my life? At school?

2. Taking my list of have-to's, what is the personal value for each "have to" that would allow me to turn them into "want to's"?

EXERCISE: Math Test

Below is a standard math test. Time yourself. You have 90 seconds to complete the test. Are you ready? Go!

8 + 2 =	7 X 2 =
9 + 11 =	9 + 2 =
4 X 3 =	8 – 4 =
9 – 3 =	9 + 6 =
7 X 4 =	8 ÷ 4 =
4 + 4 =	8 X 7 =
12 X 2 =	13 – 1 =
2 - 10 =	16 – 4 =
9 – 1 =	8 X 2 =
5 + 6 =	6 X 2 =
2 X 1 =	8 + 4 =
10 – 5 =	10 – 2 =
12 + 2 =	4 – 1 =
6 ÷ 2 =	28 + 2 =
8 + 5 =	8 + 2 =
6 + 6 =	14 ÷ 2 =

Were you able to complete the test in the time allotted? Was it relatively easy or difficult? Did you feel anxious or out of your comfort zone? Were you able to flow at your habit level? Did you feel any restrictions to operate at your potential level?

_____

_____

_____

EXERCISE: Math Test 2

Below is a standard math test. Time yourself. You have 90 seconds. This time a plus (+) sign means to multiply, a divide (÷) means to add, a minus (-) sign means to divide and a multiplication (x) sign means to subtract. Are you ready? Go!

8 + 2 =	7 X 2 =
9 + 11 =	9 + 2 =
4 X 3 =	8 − 4 =
9 − 3 =	9 + 6 =
7 X 4 =	8 ÷ 4 =
4 + 4 =	8 X 7 =
12 X 2 =	13 − 1 =
2 - 10 =	16 − 4 =
9 − 1 =	8 X 2 =
5 + 6 =	6 X 2 =
2 X 1 =	8 + 4 =
10 − 5 =	10 − 2 =
12 + 2 =	4 − 1 =
6 ÷ 2 =	28 + 2 =
8 + 5 =	8 + 2 =
6 + 6 =	14 ÷ 2 =

Were you able to complete the test in the time allotted? Was it relatively easy or difficult? Did you feel anxious or out of your comfort zone? Were you able to flow at your habit level? Did you feel any restrictions to operate at your potential level?

_____

_____

_____

EXERCISE: Have To's

Check either "Have to" or "Want to" for each of the examples below. In the empty spaces, list a few of your own activities, and whether they are "Have to" or "Want to".

HAVE TO'S		WANT TO'S
	Go to class	
	Study	
	Do homework	
	Read	
	See a tutor	
	Ask questions in class	
	Participate as part of a team	
	Give a presentation	

ARE THEY REALLY HAVE TO'S?

_____

_____

_____

_____

_____

SUMMARY: Fundamentals

You may find that you are not progressing toward your goals very fast, and wondering why, when you have written your affirmations and are continuously visualizing the end results you want. If you find yourself pulling away from the goals, there may be another reason and it has to do with information I am going to give you now.

Throughout this course, we have talked about goals being what we want. I even asked you the question, "What do you want?" What we haven't talked about is WHY we go after what we want. The "why" falls into two categories of what we call "motivation."

If what we say we want is really what someone says we should want, or it really isn't our idea, then our motivation becomes a "have to." We may feel coerced into a goal, because we should go after it, or we are being pressured into it. We can usually tell if we are being coerced by these two words – Or Else. There is some kind of terrible consequence, something too horrid to imagine, if we don't go after a goal. Our motivation is based on fear of a consequence. This coercion can come from outside of us, or it can come from inside of us.

When we live in fear, we are settling for being less than we could be. We short-change ourselves and our loved ones. When we tell ourselves that we "have to" do something, we are lowering our sense of self-esteem and our belief in our ability to make things happen for ourselves – our self-efficacy.

The key here is that when we feel like we are being pushed, anyone with any level of self-esteem will push back. This push-back can come in the form of procrastination, where we keep putting off something with every excuse in the book – and aren't those excuses easy to come up with?

We also do only enough work to get the boss, or the teacher, off of our back. We settle for mediocre grades, when we know we could do better. We just won't, because it's a "have to". Pushing back takes up an awful lot of energy, and negative energy as well. What if we switch that "have to" to a "want to?"

Putting our lives on a "want to" basis is finding the value in achievement. We choose to go after our goals because we vividly see the benefit of achieving them. We like what we are doing. In fact, we love it! With this constructive motivation, we are taking control of our decisions. We know what we are going after has value. We want it – and there is no pushing back against something that we want.

You can see why I encourage you to stop using fear on yourself. If I apply for the job, I won't get it. If I ask her for a date, I won't get it. If you play with fear, it impedes how you play. What you want to do is to see, "How good can I be?" Ask yourself, "What's the value in this?" Then, you visualize and put that kind of an emotion in.

Some of the emotion you have of fear isn't because you put it in. It's almost like you don't know how you got it. What you need to do is beat the fear or you won't let yourself take the job. You won't let yourself move away from your old friends. You won't let yourself go to school, or let yourself graduate. You just stop yourself. If you do go out socially, you just blow it because you act stupid, because you're out of your comfort zone.

You can't override your fear. You need to beat it. Let go of old, outdated beliefs. Visualize and affirm yourself into your new future – the one you decide you want.

Leave the fear behind. Put your life on a "want to, choose to, like it, love it" basis and don't look back. Take control of your decisions, and your choices. But also be willing to take accountability for those decisions and actions. Live fully into the person you are meant to be.

SUMMARY: Application

*It is my choice to change my mind, because I deserve an education, a new career,
a better income, and better opportunities for my children.*

I choose short-term sacrifices in order to reap the benefits of long-term prosperity.

*I choose to focus on where my life is going,
excited about the future that I am creating for myself.*

This is one of the hardest segments, not to understand, but to apply. Any time we find ourselves thinking:

"I have to study" or

"I have to log in" or

"I have to go to class" or

"I have to read the assignment"

 "I have to go to work"

"I have to clean the house" or

"I need a new habit or a new attitude,"

We need to stop. Why do I choose to do this? What is the benefit to me, my family, and my future?

We take control of our lives, by taking control of our mind. We choose the way we want to think about the choices we make every day. Putting life on a "choose to, want to, love to, looking forward to it" basis isn't hard when our goals, aspirations, expectations are clearly defined; when they are accurate, vivid, and we practice them every day in our mind. Remember, the excitement, attention, and focus on our goal puts the brain into action. The more vivid the goal, the more motivated we are to achieve it.

The discipline is in our own mind.

NOTES

SECTION 3: EXTENDED LEARNING

This section is designed to take you on a deeper dive into the understanding and application of the concepts.

- EL Unit 1: The Self-Talk Cycle

- EL Unit 2: The Next Time . . .

- EL Unit 3: Habits, Attitudes, Beliefs and Expectations

- EL Unit 4: Four Phases of Goal Assimilation

- EL Unit 5: Motivation In-Depth

- Conclusion

- TPSC MAS Inventory Post-Assessment

OVERVIEW

Our self-image is the accumulation of everything we believe about ourselves and our abilities. To the outer world, our self-image is reflected in our performance – what we do and how we act. What reinforces our self-image is our self-talk, which we already know we can control to build us up or tear us down. We can use this cycle to keep us the same, or help us to move to that next level in our education, our lives and careers.

OBJECTIVES

By the end of this unit, I will understand:

- my self-image is my definition of who I believe I am.

- who I believe I am is reflected in my outward performance.

- positively or negatively, my self-talk reinforces my self-image.

We act in accordance with the truth as we believe it to be.

LouTice

KEY CONCEPTS

Performance Reality: How one acts and performs based on one's currently dominant self-image.

Self-Image: The accumulation of all the attitudes and opinions one has perceived about oneself that form a subconscious picture of oneself; the imagined self; the self that one supposes oneself to be; the picture; self-regulation.

Self-Talk: An act whereby one evaluates or assesses one's behavior; how one talks or reaffirms to oneself when one reacts to one's own evaluation, or others' evaluations of one's performance. Self-talk may have an affirming influence in establishing self-image.

NOTES

Write down your ideas, observations and insights as you work through this unit. Date your entries.

....

....

....

....

....

....

....

....

....

....

....

....

....

....

....

....

....

....

....

....

REFLECTIVE QUESTIONS

1. What do I believe about my abilities to succeed as a student on the road to graduation?

2. What actions or behaviors do I show to those around me that reflect these beliefs?

3. How does my self-talk support these beliefs?

4. What do I want to change to help move me along toward my graduation?

THOUGHT PATTERNS FOR A SUCCESSFUL CAREER®
Mastering the Attitude of Success™ • Participant Manual
©The Pacific Institute®, LLC

EXERCISE: The Self-Talk Cycle

Get out a test, or a project, or an assignment from earlier in the term. Review how the self-talk cycle applies to each phase.

What is my current self-image regarding test taking, interviewing, trusting teachers, accepting help from classmates, my capabilities of being able to do this coursework? What are the significant events that have impacted my self-image? Is my present self-image helping me to release my potential, or not? Does my self-image need to be changed?

SELF-IMAGE

SELF-TALK

PERFORMANCE REALITY

In order to intercept my self-talk and begin to create the new replacement picture in my mind, what would my new affirmation be? (Refer to the affirmation guidelines in Unit 10 to write your affirmation in first-person, present tense, experiential or positive imagery. Remember, I x V = R in order to change the picture on the subconscious level.)

Based on my self-image with regard to today, do my behaviors and performance match my self-image? What would my behaviors look like, feel like, be like if I were behaving closer to my potential?

5 COLUMN AFFIRMATION WRITING GUIDE

Directions: Working from left to right, create an effective affirmation for each example.

Current Reality Present State	Potential Loss Emotion-Feeling	Vision Desired State	Why? Personal Value Emotion-Feeling	Affirmation Personal-Positive-Clear Balance-Action-Emotion I xV = R
A statement describing the "now."	What is the "now" cost-ing you? • Effect on you • Feeling	What does it look like without the problem?	What does that desired state "give" me?	
I do not like taking tests.				
I am terrible at interviewing!				
It is hard for me to trust teachers.				

SUMMARY: Fundamentals

Let's review a little bit, and then move forward. We've gone through a great deal of material up to this point.

You and I have what we call a self-image. That self-image is really nothing made up. It is your reality that's stored in the neurons of your brain. That self-image controls how you act or how you behave. We call that how your Performance Reality actually is.

Now, what does that mean, performance reality? It is how you really are if you are not faking it. So your self-image automatically controls "you." Now, you can override it. You can try hard to be better, sweeter, nicer, friendlier, or happier. But inside, you know "if I let go of control, they'd see the real me." This is the "real me" we are talking about.

What we're saying really is, as I think, I am. As I think, I am. Now, this controls your automatic, free flowing behavior of the way you automatically act. What caused that to occur in the first place was how you spoke to yourself with your self-talk. Remember, self-talk is that three dimensional form of thought: words, pictures, and emotion. The word for self-talk might be called by others an affirmation.

Now, what's an affirmation? It's just a statement of fact, a statement of belief. You are making thousands of them every day: I like this. I don't like that. That's like me. That's not like me. You are constantly talking to yourself.

That self-talk forms your self-image and still does. What makes it difficult for us to change is every time you make a mistake, and you see yourself making a fool of yourself, messing up some way, and so on, as you observe how you messed up, you tell yourself, "Well, that's always been like me." So remember, your self-talk goes like this: "That's like me. I've always been a screw up." "I've always made a fool of myself." "I've always been forgetful." "That's normal for me." "That's like me." This self-talk reinforces your already existing self-image that isn't good enough for you, anymore.

SUMMARY: Application – Taking Tests

Think about taking tests or exams. What feelings do you get? Are the feelings negative, positive, or neutral? Your answer provides insight into your self-image with regard to test-taking.

If they are positive, that's great. Positive thoughts/emotions toward test-taking become an asset when it comes to preparation – studying, keeping your attention, focusing on what you need to learn, continuing to work through content that might not be coming as easy to you, seeking out help if necessary and ultimately walking into the test confident and self-assured because you expect to do well. Why? Because you know that you are ready. Because of the positive self-image, you have put yourself in a position to succeed and release your potential at the highest level. It is the self-image, the picture of how you see you, that gives you the drive, energy, problem-solving and creativity to ready yourself for the test. Your self-image of seeing yourself performing at a high level when taking tests releases your actions and behaviors to do the work to prepare that supports the self-image.

What if the thought of taking a test is wrapped up in negative emotions? Just the thought can make you nervous, anxious and make your stomach turn. You begin to sweat. Your mind starts racing toward thoughts of how you might be able to get out of it by taking the test at a later date. If it really frightens you, you may begin wondering, "How bad would my life be if I just gave up getting an education altogether?"

How do you think you got such a negative self-image with regard to test-taking in the first place? Obviously, those emotions didn't appear by accident. You have a few, if not many, very negative, debilitating emotions. That picture shows itself every time you perceive, "I have to take a test." The picture is real. It may come with awful memories of embarrassment, or teasing and humiliation from other students. It could be criticism from teachers or family members. Very likely, it is the nail in the coffin, the final straw.

A negative affirmation from a significant person to whom you gave heavy sanction, which means you "accepted and assimilated" their point of view, became a part of your self-image. That person was a "who-said" in your life because of the way you perceived them. They could have been a teacher, a counselor, a school administrator, or a parent, older sibling, grandparent, close friend. It could have been a coach or leader in your community. Regardless of their role in your life, you gave them sanction because of who they were and what they represented at that moment of your life.

As a result of all those negative emotions, you now have a self-image that says, "I don't, I can't, I won't take tests. I'm not good at them." "It never turns out well." With your self-talk, you are reaffirming the self-image that is holding you back from releasing your potential to take tests well. You keep reminding yourself of the person you are, not the person you are capable of being.

Here's the good news. By intercepting your self-talk you can begin to tell yourself the person you intend to be. You need to begin giving yourself a replacement picture of the new you successfully taking tests. The new image is what it would look like, feel like, and be like when you are effectively taking tests.

SUMMARY: Application – Interviewing

Think about interviewing for a new job. Think about your self-image with regard to speaking clearly, confidently and articulating your skills and abilities to a potential employer. As you consider the self-talk cycle, what is your current self-image? If you think about performing in an interview, is it at the level you want or do you need to change your self-image?

What if the thought of interviewing makes you nervous, anxious, or even frightened, taking you way out of your comfort zone? How do you think you got that self-image in the first place? Perhaps it was unsuccessful job interviews in the past or one-on-one confrontational meetings with teachers, school administrators, coaches, supervisors, or managers. Regardless of what happened, it was through some type of negative past experience. It may have happened once, or many times. Either way, you played the negative experience or experiences over and over in your mind with the negative emotion until it became a part of your historical memory. It became your self-image with regard to interviewing. Based on this, how are you going to act when sitting in an interview? Your mind goes blank. Words don't come out, and when they do you can't seem to put a sentence together. You sweat through your clothes. Your stomach starts churning, and you blow the interview.

On your way home from the interview, you reflect, "I've never been able to do that. How am I going to ever get a job if I can't interview? I might as well not even go to the next one. I already know how it's going to turn out." With your self-talk you are reaffirming the self-image that is holding you back. You keep reminding yourself of the person you are.

By intercepting your self-talk you begin to tell yourself the person you intend to be. You begin giving yourself a replacement picture of the new you in a successful interview. The new image is what it would look like, feel like, be like when you are interviewing effectively. Your affirmation might be something like, "I am calm, confident, and articulate when speaking about my talents and abilities to perform in this job because I am qualified, prepared, and deserve a new career."

Remember, the affirmation, the new picture you are painting in your mind, is not the end result. It is the means to get you the end result. Remember, you read the affirmation, get a picture of you sitting in an actual interview, and feel the positive emotions of being calm, confident, and articulate. The greater the image, the more drive you get to do something about it.

The more you see yourself performing at your new level of expectation, the more you practice answering questions. You rehearse in front of a mirror. You ask your friends or family to interview you. You continually work with career services to sharpen all aspects of the job attainment process. As you change the construct in your mind (the calm, confident, articulate interviewer who deserves a new career), you become discontent with the old self-image. You grow yourself into a fabulous interviewer by first changing your mind from what you used to be, which then releases your potential to grow into the new you.

NOTES

THOUGHT PATTERNS FOR A SUCCESSFUL CAREER®
Mastering the Attitude of Success™ • Participant Manual
©The Pacific Institute®, LLC

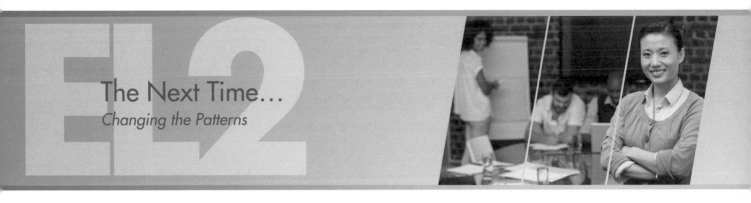

EL2

The Next Time...
Changing the Patterns

OVERVIEW

As we move from goal-setting to goal-assimilating, it is all about the replacement pictures of what it is we intend. It is about what we expect vs. our current reality. On the road to graduation, it is vital to make immediate course corrections in our minds when we find ourselves falling away from our goals. We want to coach ourselves forward, rather than backward, and we do that through the discipline of controlling our self-talk.

OBJECTIVES

By the end of this unit, I will understand:

- why I need to give myself replacement pictures to help me determine my future.

- if I change what I think about, I can largely determine what happens to me.

- there is a process to self-correct and focus on the future I want.

Stop it! I'm better than that. The next time, I intend to...

LouTice

KEY CONCEPTS

Attitude: A consciously held belief or opinion; easiest to visualize if we picture ourselves leaning toward those things we like (positive) and away from those things we dislike (negative).

Habit: A learned act; a pattern of activity that has, through repetition, become automatic, fixed, and easily and effortlessly carried out.

Self-Talk: An act whereby one evaluates or assesses one's behavior; how one talks or reaffirms to oneself when one reacts to one's own evaluation, or others' evaluations of one's performance. Self-talk may have an affirming influence in establishing self-image.

The next time . . .: A vow to better performance at the next opportunity.

NOTES

Write down your ideas, observations and insights as you work through this unit. Date your entries.

REFLECTIVE QUESTIONS

1. If I move toward what I think about, what do I want for my future?

2. Based on what I want, what adjustments do I need to make to my self-talk and self-image in order to be successful?

3. What behavior do I want to stop today, and what does my "next time" replacement picture look like?

EXERCISE: The Power in the Replacement Picture

When we interrupt our self-talk, we still need to give ourselves a replacement picture to move toward. In the examples below, coaching yourself forward, create the words you will give yourself for "the next time," and create the picture those words will inspire.

COACHING MYSELF FORWARD

SITUATION (FOR ME)	THE NEXT TIME, I INTEND TO...(THE ACTION/BEHAVIOR I INTEND TO CHANGE)	REPLACEMENT PICTURE: WHAT DO I INTEND TO DWELL ON MOVING FORWARD? (WHAT WILL IT LOOK LIKE WHEN IT'S "FIXED"?)
Skipping an assignment		
Doing poorly on a test		
Stumbling through a presentation		
"Yelling" at my child		
Argument with my parent or significant other		

EXERCISE: The Power in the Replacement Picture, cont.

Now that we are good at interrupting our own self-talk, we can help those around us do the same. In the examples below, coaching others forward, create the words you will give yourself for "the next time," and create the picture those words will inspire.

COACHING OTHERS FORWARD

SITUATION (FOR OTHERS)	THE NEXT TIME, I INTEND TO...(THE ACTION/BEHAVIOR I INTEND TO HELP CHANGE)	REPLACEMENT PICTURE: WHAT PICTURE CAN YOU HELP CREATE TO HELP MOVE SOMEONE FORWARD?
My child does poorly on a test		
My child gets in a conflict or argument at school		
My friend has a poor job interview		
My friend fails a test		
My friend is missing to many classes		

REMEMBER: It is the power of the replacement picture that provides the energy to change the behavior in the first place!

THOUGHT PATTERNS FOR A SUCCESSFUL CAREER®
Mastering the Attitude of Success™ • Participant Manual
©The Pacific Institute®, LLC

EXERCISE: "Time-out" and More

In order to change Habits, Attitudes, or Beliefs that might be getting in the way of "coaching" ourselves and others forward, we want to bring situations to conscious awareness. We choose to say or do something differently. In the situations below, how will you handle the situation "the next time..."?

1. When you are dealing with children, either your own or another's, how did the Application example resonate with you? How will you change or adjust how you handle that situation?

    _____

    _____

2. How might you talk with your children about cleaning their rooms or keeping their bathroom clean?

    _____

    _____

3. How might you work with children in regard to how they talk to each other?

    _____

    _____

4. How might you approach a teacher or instructor differently if you are unhappy with a grade?

    _____

    _____

5. How might you approach a colleague, supervisor, or manager differently when a situation arises at work?

    _____

    _____

SUMMARY: Fundamentals

Let's talk about the process of making changes to the habits, attitudes, beliefs and expectations that are necessary to attain the goals you have set for yourself. It is so important to be clear, accurate, and have an exact picture of what it is that you intend – what it is that you expect – in order to move in that direction. The challenge is that the most dominant picture in your mind currently is not the one you intend, but one you have, based on the past. You are working on your brain – through focus, attention, and the constant reviewing of your progress – to make sure that the new habit, attitude, or belief takes hold so the autopilot changes in the direction of your expectation.

Let's focus on evaluating your progress toward the changes you intend to make. By having proper focus and attention on the goal, the brain will provide the drive, energy, problem-solving and creativity. These are the "how" you are going to get there. It is not magic. It is focus and attention. Being honest and most likely realistic, you are going to fall back to your old thoughts, old habits or old beliefs – especially in times when we have unusual stress, additional responsibilities, or disruptions in the normal flow of our routines.

I want you to say to yourself, when you make a mistake, "That's not like me. I'm better than that." Now, not actually up to this point, because you can start arguing with yourself, "Who are you kidding? I've been like this since I was four!" "I was like this yesterday, and I'm telling myself it's not like me?" You want to say to yourself, "That is no longer who I am. I'm much better than that." What you need to tell yourself then is, "The next time..." That's the key phrase. "The next time, I intend to..." and you go on to tell yourself what you intend to do.

"The next time, I intend to think before I talk." "The next time, I intend to control my temper." "The next time, I intend to..." Do you understand? Otherwise, if you don't do that, your self-talk goes, "What's the matter with me anyway? How could I have been so stupid?" Then you get caught in that stream of negative self-talk, describing to yourself what's wrong with you. Do you ever do that? It's like, "There I go again. What's the matter with me? I've always been that way." This hardens the self-image, which makes sure you behave like that the rest of your life – until you change it.

Good athletes don't dwell on their mistakes. Great athletes quickly make the correction in their minds. Remember, it's all about replacement pictures. You want to give yourself a replacement picture for the way you're behaving now. This is all about giving yourself replacement pictures for your social life, for your personal life, for how you feel about yourself, how you think about yourself. It's how you want to live. It is about how much money you want to accumulate. It's whether you see yourself as poor or wealthy, seeing yourself as smart or dumb.

It's all about a replacement picture, and the key phrase for the replacement picture is, "The next time..." It shuts off the negative self-talk, if you tell yourself what you're going to do the next time.

A key ingredient in making changes you desire is the evaluation of your progress. With each success, each positive step in the direction of your goal, you need to assimilate that positive movement. Use that evidence to build your efficacy. Remember, building efficacy comes from taking ownership and accountability for what it is that you are causing. When you fall back, or revert to an old way of thinking, which results in the old way of behaving, you need to stop and correct the process in your mind.

The Blue Angels is the United States Navy's flight demonstration squadron. After every flight exhibition, they conduct what they call an After Action Review. As a part of that process, all the members of the flight team have the same expectation. It's not about egos. It's not about fixing the blame or accusing others. They "'fess it and fix it." Each member tells the team what he did wrong and what he intends to do the next time to correct it. They don't dwell on the mistake. They dwell on what they are going to do to correct it moving forward. Why do they think this is so important? They choose to focus on doing it right, turning the mind's attention to the right way, not the wrong. They constantly evaluate their progress toward the perfect flight demonstration.

SUMMARY: Application

How familiar are you with the disciplinary technique of Timeout? After you have placed the child in timeout, what is it that you ask the child to think about while he or she is in Timeout?

The most common response from parents or caregivers is, "I want you think about what you just did." Why do you think that most caregivers would send the child off into timeout with that instruction? Because that instruction has been assimilated from being given the same instruction as a child. Or by observing others, siblings or friends or relatives, when they gave that instruction to a child heading into timeout.

When I assume the role of caregiver and it is my responsibility to discipline a child, I may accidently fall into the habitual flow and give this child the same instruction. "I want you to think about what you just did." The instruction flows out of habit, based on what I have assimilated from the world around me.

Is that really what we want the child to focus on? Wouldn't it be better to ask the child what he should do "the next time" that situation occurs? In other words, do I really want the child to focus on his misbehavior or would I rather ask the child to focus on an alternative solution, a better way of handling that situation.

Apply the same to yourself. When you make a mistake, screw up a project, get a test score below your capability, miss an assignment, or let someone down, do you tend to dwell on what you did wrong? Instead, focus on what you intend to do to correct the situation. Learn to coach yourself forward just like you would someone else. By giving that child the instruction of what he/she intends to do the next time, you are coaching the child forward. You need to be able to do that for yourself also. It all begins with becoming aware of, and then controlling, your own self-talk.

NOTES

Habits, Attitudes, Beliefs, and Expectations
Essentials for a Successful Career

OVERVIEW

We have assimilated our habits, attitudes, beliefs and our expectations of the world around us throughout our lifetime. They are predominantly automatic, as they reside in our subconscious mind, and they define "normal" for us. A lot of our "HABEs" were established when we were very young, and without further reflection, have remained the same ever since. However, if we want to change and grow, we need to examine which of our habits, attitudes and beliefs still work for us, and which ones need to be changed because they are holding us back.

OBJECTIVES

By the end of this unit, I will understand:

- I regulate my behavior at my belief level.

- how to recognize when a habit, attitude or belief is holding me back.

- I get what I expect, not necessarily what I want.

We self-regulate at the level of our beliefs, not at the level of our potential.

LouTice

KEY CONCEPTS

Attitude: A consciously held belief or opinion; easiest to visualize if we picture ourselves leaning toward those things we like (positive) and away from those things we dislike (negative).

Belief: An emotional acceptance of a proposition, statement, or doctrine.

Expectation: The prospect of a future embodiment of an abstract idea; an anticipation.

Habit: A learned act; a pattern of activity that has, through repetition, become automatic, fixed, and easily and effortlessly carried out.

NOTES

Write down your ideas, observations and insights as you work through this unit. Date your entries.

REFLECTIVE QUESTIONS

1. This is one current habit, that I know is holding me back, and I want to change it:

   This is what I want my new habit to look like:

2. Is my current attitude toward attendance, or logging on to my online courses, doing homework or the required reading moving me to my goal of graduation or away from it? Why?

3. Where in my life do I notice people respond to me, based on the person I believe myself to be?

4. Listed here are two of my classes this term. For each, what do I expect to get out of them, that will help me move toward graduation?

THOUGHT PATTERNS FOR A SUCCESSFUL CAREER®
Mastering the Attitude of Success™ • Participant Manual
©The Pacific Institute®, LLC

PART 1: HABITS
REFLECTIVE QUESTIONS

1. What new habits do I need to directly ensure my success in education?

2. What are potential habits that will help my academics and my career?

3. What habits do I need to improve my personal life?

EXERCISE: Balancing My Life Habit Loop

Working to achieve our education and graduation, we want to keep balance in our life, as well. In the far left column are some important parts to a happy life. Work each one through the Cue, Behavior and Reward that will help create a new habit. Be sure to add to the list of new habits you want to create, as you work through this exercise.

NEW HABIT	What is the Cue, the Trigger that will launch me into the new behavior? Is it a specific time? Is it immediately following a specific event or action?	What is the new Behavior, that I intend to Repeat, until it becomes Automatic (able to be performed without conscious thought)?	What is my Reward for repeating the behavior? Why am I going to be willing to keep doing it until it becomes automatic?
Study			
Attendance			
Saving money			
Quality time with family			
Exercise			

[Habit Loops adapted from the work of Charles DuHigg (2012).]

THOUGHT PATTERNS FOR A SUCCESSFUL CAREER®
Mastering the Attitude of Success™ • Participant Manual
©The Pacific Institute®, LLC

SUMMARY: Fundamentals — Habits

Writer David Foster Wallace offers, "There are these two young fish swimming along and they happen to meet an older fish swimming the other way, who nods at them and says 'Morning, boys. How's the water?' And the two young fish swim on for a bit, and then eventually one of them looks over at the other and asks, 'What's water?'" Charles DuHigg, the author of *The Power of Habit* describes the water as our habits, the unthinking choices and invisible decisions that surround us every day— and which, just by looking at them, we can see through our scotomas and they become visible again. What makes us want to look at those habits again? That would be a new goal.

Habits emerge because the brain is constantly looking for ways to save effort. Because habits allow our minds to be more efficient, our brain will try to make almost any routine into a habit. In fact, research out of Duke University found that more than 40% of the actions people perform each day aren't actual decisions, but habits. [Duhigg, Charles, *The Power of Habit: Why We Do What We Do in Life and Business* (page 2).] Habits are actual changes in the brain chemistry creating neurological cravings within the brain.

Habits can emerge outside our consciousness, or can be deliberately designed. We develop habits by both accident and intent. By accident means outside of consciousness, like cracking your knuckles, chewing your nails, playing with your hair, or using "um" as a transition when speaking. By intent means there is deliberate coordination. Athletes, artists, dancers, musicians – all of their actions operate free-flowingly without having to think, because they have been habituated. How did their actions develop to the point of flowing freely? It was the willingness to practice, practice, practice, and repeat, repeat, repeat until the action became automatic at a very high level.

How was it possible for them or for us to create the habit? We need a clearly defined goal, a vivid image of the intention, and a high expectation of the result. Think of all the habits we have developed by intent, like riding a bike, driving a car, playing video games, or mastering the countless apps on our smartphones. Because we desire the result, we are willing to put in the work. We practice, practice, practice, and repeat, repeat, repeat. When we approach behaviors with a want to, choose to, I like it, I love it frame of mind, it is easy to muster the drive, energy, passion and motivation we need to develop the habit. Our brain creates it for us because we want it that way.

Consider the "conditions" that exist in order for a habit to take hold. First, habits are behaviors, an action, something we do. (They can also be thought patterns, as we'll see when we get into attitudes). Second, the behavior is practiced and repeated over and over, until it becomes...Third, subconscious in nature. It is automatic and performed without conscious thought or needing a conscious decision. It is through the deliberate process of setting and assimilating goals that we can begin to develop the habits necessary to successfully complete the goal. Because of the vivid image of our intention, of what we expect of ourselves, we have the willingness to develop new habits and possibly get rid of some old ones.

SUMMARY: Application — Habit Loops

In order to deliberately create habits, we need to delve further into what constitutes a habit and then how we assimilated them. Charles DuHigg, in *The Power of Habit,* does a great job of compiling and interpreting the prevailing research about how we can intentionally put habit loops into place.

A habit loop consists of three parts: A Cue (which is a trigger), something subconscious or conscious that tips us into the second part, the Routine. The Routine is an action or behavior that is repeated free-flowingly, without needing conscious thought or conscious decision-making. Why we are willing to work the routine until it becomes automatic is the Reward, the satisfaction, the sense of accomplishment that is directly tied to the performance of the Routine. We need to determine the WIIFM (What's In It For Me) if we truly desire to create a new Habit.

Duhigg advises you must decide to change, to change the habit. You must consciously accept the hard work of identifying the cues and rewards that drive the habits' routines, and then find alternatives. You must know you have control and be self-conscious enough to use it. Almost all the other patterns that exist in most people's lives – how we eat and sleep and talk to our kids, how we unthinkingly spend our time, attention, and money – those are habits that we know exist. Once you understand that habits can change, you have the freedom – and the responsibility – to remake them. Once you understand that habits can be rebuilt, the power of habit becomes easier to grasp, and the only option left is to get to work.

From a neurological standpoint, what keeps us moving toward our goals in life comes down to the mind's ability to remind us of how satisfied we will feel when we accomplish those things (a capacity residing in the circuitry between the amygdala and the left prefrontal lobe of the brain). No matter what drives our passion to do our best work – whether it's the pure excitement it brings, the satisfaction of learning to do something better, or simply the money we earn – all the rewards share a common neural pathway. Passion for doing the work, in the brain, means that circuits linked to the left prefrontal cortex pump out a fairly steady stream of good feeling as we perform the routine. [Goleman, Boyatzis and McKee, *Primal Leadership: Unleashing the Power of Emotional Intelligence,* (2013)]

Our brains crave familiarity in music because familiarity is how we manage to hear without becoming distracted by all the sound. Just as the scientists at MIT discovered that behavioral habits prevent us from becoming overwhelmed by the endless decisions we would otherwise have to make each day, listening habits exist, because without them, it would be impossible to determine if we should concentrate on our child's voice, the coach's whistle, or the noise from a busy street during a Saturday soccer game. Listening habits allow us to unconsciously separate important noises from those that can be ignored. That's why songs that sound "familiar" – even if you've never heard them before – are sticky. Our brains are designed to prefer auditory patterns that seem similar to what we've already heard. [Duhigg, Charles, *The Power of Habit: Why We Do What We Do in Life and Business* (page 202).]

How powerful can habits be? How can our habits, the willingness to put in the work, drive us to the point of mastery? Psychologist K. Anders Ericsson and colleagues studied master violinists. Top concert violinists could easily rack up 10,000 hours of grueling practice by the time they were twenty years old, practicing more than thirty hours per week. By contrast, they found that students who were merely exceptional studied only 8,000 hours or fewer. Future music teachers practiced about a total of 4,000 hours. [Kaku, Michio, *The Future of the Mind: The Scientific Quest to Understand, Enhance and Empower the Mind* (Kindle location 2398 of 6516)]

Therefore, in order to have successful habits incorporated into ourselves, we need to be willing to put in the time and effort to make it happen.

(For more habit loop applications, view the Study Habit Loop and Online Attendance Habit Loop video segments that go with this unit.)

PART 2: ATTITUDES
REFLECTIVE QUESTIONS

1. When I have a positive attitude toward the completion of a task:

   • how does it feel?

   • how many of my thoughts during the day are focused on that task?

   • how much time do I devote to the behaviors that take me toward the completion of that task?

2. When I have a negative attitude toward the completion of a task:

   • how does it feel?

   • how many of my thoughts during the day are focused on that task?

   • how much time do I devote to the behaviors that take me toward the completion of that task?

3. When I have a negative attitude toward the completion of a task, do I have certain techniques that I apply to "get around" my attitude?

EXERCISE: Attitudes – Leaning Toward or Leaning Away?

Are my attitudes getting in my way? In the table below, for each situation, check the appropriate box – Toward or Away. Then, reflect on Why I lean toward or away. Finally, write down what I want to do in order to move closer to my goals.

Leaning Toward	SITUATION	Leaning Away	WHY?	What do I want to change to move toward my goals?
	Attending Class or Logging in			
	Completing homework assignments on time			
	Reading Assignments			
	Participating in class discussions			
	Research for writing assignments			
	Balancing home, work, family, school			
	Adjusting TV time or social time to focus on school			

SUMMARY: Fundamentals — Attitudes

When we set a goal, our attitudes toward that goal are evoked inside of us. Attitudes that are taking us toward our goal, we call positive because they cause us to lean in. Attitudes that are taking us away from our goal, we call negative because they leaning us away from our goal. Why is this so important? Because attitudes have everything to do with the release of your potential.

If we have a negative attitude, we tend to disengage, lose energy and drive. We creatively avoid doing things necessary to achieve the goal. We come up with excuses as to why it won't work or why it can't be done. On the other hand, a positive attitude releases just the opposite inside of us – the drive, energy, desire, motivation, excitement, and passion that allow us to do the work to achieve the goal.

If you have kids (or maybe if you just think about how you acted when you were a kid), think about the difference in the release of potential when you tell your kids (or you were told) to do the dishes. Later, upon completion, you find (or your parents found) all the dishes clean, but not the pots, pans, or silverware. Why? Because you didn't specifically tell them wash those. A negative attitude lead to the avoidance of all the items that weren't dishes.

If the thought of the new goal elicits negative attitudes, we must change the attitude in order to smoothly move into our goal. Therefore, you may want to ask yourself, "Is my present attitude toward attendance, or logging in to my online class, or doing homework, or reading the course materials or participating in class discussions taking me toward my goal of graduation or away from it?"

SUMMARY: APPLICATIONS — ATTITUDES

How do you feel about reading your assignments? You will get plenty of things to read during the course of your education. When you get a reading assignment, if you like reading and enjoy it, then your attitude is working for you. It releases your potential to read and your attitude isn't in the way. Because you like it, you keep doing what you need to do until you understand the material and complete the assignment.

But if you have a negative attitude, your picture is very different. You don't enjoy it. You don't like it. Reading feels more like a have to, rather than a want to. Because of your negative attitude, you find yourself engaging in creative avoidance. You find all kinds of chores and other things that need to be done instead of reading. Even if you do "force" yourself to read, you don't get much out of it – not because you aren't capable, but more likely, because you're wrestling with your negative attitude. You have the potential to read, the capability of understanding the material, but your attitude is really getting in the way of the release of that potential. Keep in mind, you are fully capable. It's a negative attitude in the way.

How often do you read every day? How many emails, text messages, tweets, instant messages, websites, and other electronic communications, magazines, newspapers, etc., might you read during your day? You probably read thousands, if not tens of thousands, of words every day. What releases our potential to read them? Your attitude. Once you are capable of reading, then it is your attitude that has everything to do with the release of that potential. If your attitude is holding you back from reading your course assignments, you may want to consider changing that attitude to the same one that allows you to release your potential to read text messages, emails, tweets, instant messages, etc.

When we stay focused on our goals and keep in front of us the reasons why we intend to do something, it is easy to influence our attitude. If not, we are stuck with the one we have and it may not be taking us in the direction that we intend.

PART 3: BELIEFS
REFLECTIVE QUESTIONS

1. Listed below are what I consider my core beliefs. They define me as I intend to be, and won't be changed without a very good reason.

2. These are the behaviors that reflect my core beliefs:

EXERCISE: Beliefs and Goal Achievement

For this exercise, we are going to use information from earlier exercises and dig a little deeper to ensure we reach the goals we have set for ourselves. Please refer to your responses in Unit 4: The "Truth" is What We Believe It Is (Balance Wheel exercise) and Unit 9: Setting Benchmarks for My Future (Balance Wheel Drill Down and Mini Bucket List).

WHAT IS THE GOAL? (refer to U4 and U9 exercises)	What is my current belief with regard to accomplishing the goal?	If this belief is in the way, why do I still believe it?	What do I want to believe in order to reach my goal?

SUMMARY: Fundamentals — Beliefs

Now, so it is the quality and quantity of reality stored in your subconscious that the creative subconscious makes happen in your life all the time. Change the quality and quantity in the subconscious, and your life gets better all the time. Is it outside me or is it inside me is the question? Is it outside me or is it inside me? If you don't know how your mind works, you know what you do? You keep waiting to win the lottery. You keep waiting for people or something outside of you to happen that will change life for the better.

What if you knew that if you changed the quality in here your life gets better? That's good news, because you can control that. You can't control whether the world outside is going to find and discover you and make you a superstar. But because you're going to change your mind, you will become a superstar. There is a direct relationship between the quality of the picture in your subconscious and the way life goes out here.

One of Lou's adopted children is in grade school and the kids picked on him. He went to junior high school. Darn the bad luck, the kids picked on him, even though he was big and strong. Then he went to a new high school where nobody knew him, and guess what? People picked on him. Then he went in the Army, and the sergeant picked on him. He got out of the Army, got his first job at a fast food place and the boss picked on him. Can you imagine the bad luck?

His parents got him a tow truck business and hired the former owner to mentor and take care of things until he got the business going. It was about six weeks into the business, he comes home and he says, "I quit." Lou's response? "Why?" "Bill's picking on me." Lou said, "Man, you can't quit. You own the business!"

Do you think this was a string of bad luck? Possibly, but he had been abused as a young child, so he kept letting people do that. Your body language betrays what you believe about you in how you stand, how you talk, how you hold yourself. It's all subconscious. If you don't change your mind, your life keeps repeating itself. People act towards you as they see you. If you look like and think you're shy, they treat you like you're shy. People do respond to you based upon how they perceive you. Your body language is constantly telling them how to treat you. You change your internal belief, and you'll be surprised how the people outside of you change.

SUMMARY: Application — Beliefs

Our beliefs can include our morals, values, ethics – all the "truths" that we have come to know about us, the world around us, and our place in it. A timeless psychological principle suggests that as human beings we behave and act at our belief level, not necessarily our potential level. Henry Ford famously explained it as, "If you think you can or you think you can't, you're right."

Neuropsychologist Donald Hebb summed up the formation of the neural circuitry in our brain succinctly in what has become known as Hebb's Law: "Neurons that fire together wire together." This is the physiological basis for how our neural pathways control our automatic behaviors when we're not consciously controlling them. The neural pathways we develop from our experiences (and our interpretations of them) have become our autopilot. Therefore, the firing of neurons along these neural pathways cause our behavior at the subconscious level. [Fogel, Steven Jay; Rosin, Mark (2014-03-06). Kindle Locations 878-882).]

Why is this so significant? We can have dozens if not hundreds of neural pathways that our subconscious uses to control our behaviors that have been programmed by accident, not by intent. We are responding in the present not based on the situation as it is, the reality as it is in front of us right now, but rather based on how we have hardwired our brain to respond from our past experiences.

British pediatric neurologist Andrew Curran's explanation of the way these neural pathways are formed in childhood is significant to how controlling these pathways can be throughout our lifetime. When a child is complimented by parents (or significant people in their lives) on what they consider good behavior, our brain releases a chemical called dopamine, a neurotransmitter. This chemical messenger shoots from one neuron to another across a juncture called a synapse. The dopamine encourages the formation of the neural pathway that causes that particular behavior, and through this process, the "hardwiring" for the behavior becomes stronger. [Fogel, Steven Jay; Rosin, Mark (2014-03-06). (Kindle Locations 872-876).]

However, what happens when a traumatic event occurs, when we have a negative interpretation of an event? When the amygdala (at the heart of our emotional center) responds to a present situation based on an autopilot misinterpretation of an event, our behavior will always be inappropriate because the amygdala and our hard-wiring aren't responding to the present event as it is actually happening now. It is responding with an old interpretation of what it considers a similar past event. [Fogel, Steven Jay; Rosin, Mark (2014-03-06). (Kindle Locations 841-844).]

We have assimilated our beliefs from the world around us – by whom we were raised, the family, friends, and community around us; where we were raised; on the playgrounds and schools and sports fields, churches, and community centers, and through what was deemed important within our core group (education, religion, politics, etc.). Because we are taught, guided, coached by people who raise us, care for us, look out for us, feed us, clothe us, they have significant influence on us. So as they teach, coach, and mentor we tend to sanction what it is they are teaching, which means we agree with it.

Then, through repetition and practice over years and years, we assimilate it and it becomes a part of us. For the most part, those beliefs have served us pretty well throughout our lifetime. However, some have not. We may need to change and challenge previously held beliefs that are holding us back from where we intend to be.

How do we know which ones need to be changed or challenged? That's why clear, defined, vivid goals are essential. It's the goal that allows us to "inventory" the beliefs, the habits, the attitudes (some of that hardwiring) that aren't consistent or congruent with the new expectation we have set for ourselves.

PART 4: EXPECTATIONS
REFLECTIVE QUESTIONS

1. It what areas of my life might the self-fulfilling prophecy apply?

2. What is the mindset I intend to have when I wake up each morning?

3. What is it that I expect of myself each and every day?

EXERCISE: Expectations From My Course Schedule

Prior to each term, list your course schedule. Then, decide what you are going to expect of yourself from each class. Are there any adjustments you want to make in your expectation? How will you guard against self-correction backwards?

CLASS SCHEDULE	What do I expect of myself from this class?	What changes or adjustments do I want to make in order to achieve my expectation?	How do I "guard against" subconscious self-correction as I near my expectation?

By raising what it is that I expect of myself, I get the energy to change, adjust, or modify my habits, attitudes, or beliefs necessary to reach what I expect.

SUMMARY: Fundamentals — Expectations

What is it that you expect of yourself? When you think about your education, what is it that you expect? Do you expect to graduate? Do you expect perfect attendance? Do you expect to study, to work hard? Do you expect to challenge yourself to learn even difficult subjects? Do you expect to graduate with Honors?

Or, do you just expect to slide by, only expect to meet the minimum requirements for attendance and grades, only expect to do the necessary work to pass the class and no more?

We need to think of our expectations in terms of another timeless psychological principle, the self-fulfilling prophecy. If we expect a bad day, go figure, we have one. If we expect to get nervous giving a presentation, go figure, we get nervous. If you expect that the next 50 minutes of class to be boring and dull, go figure why you can't get your head off the desk.

It is the expectation that we have that drives us to do or not do the things that would be necessary to achieve the result. If we are eagerly looking forward to the day and expect it to be fun, go figure when it is fun. If we expect to be confident and articulate when giving a presentation, go figure why we are. If you go to class with the expectation to learn and make it interesting, go figure why you're alert, attentive, participate, and ask questions.

The act of goal-setting and raising what we expect of ourselves is an intentional and deliberate process. When we see ourselves performing or achieving at a certain level and we look at the truth as it currently is and we're not there, it creates the energy, drive, and motivation to fix, resolve, or work toward the goal.

SUMMARY: Application — Expectations

You get your schedule and look at the list of classes. There it is, that one course that you have dreaded for as long as you can remember. It may be the very course that kept you from starting school long before now. Let's say it's a math course. Now, why are you dreading it? Well maybe because you have a mountain of transcripts that show poor grades in math. Maybe it's because of nightmares of being embarrassed or humiliated in front of your peers because you just couldn't get it. Therefore, what do you expect of yourself as you begin the class? Probably, not much. Perhaps you expect the class to be boring, to feel like torture on the level of a root canal. Maybe, you just hope to get by with a C average or even just pass would be good enough.

But let's say you decide to put forth the effort. You go to class, read the chapters, complete the practice problems and all the assignments. You ask questions, seek further instruction when you don't understand a concept, and participate in a study group. You study, study, study prior to the first exam. As a result of all your preparation, you do very well, far above your initial expectation – maybe even 90%+ or an A.

What do you think will happen on the next test, if you fail to consciously raise the level of what you expect of yourself? Your subconscious mind helps you self-regulate at your belief level, your current level of expectation, and not necessarily your potential level. You will fall back into your old habits through subconscious self-correction. Do you know what goes through the mind of a C student who gets an A? "Now I can fail the next two tests and still get my C. I can still pass the class!"

Therefore, you must consciously take control and ask yourself, "If I had the potential to get the A on the first test, then maybe I have the potential to do the same on the next one?" But how? You do it by raising what you expect of yourself. By doing so, you become more willing to do all the same things you did in preparation for the first test on the next one. Rather than building a scotoma to all the things you did to cause the first A, you "see" all the things you did to cause the A in the first place and do them all again.

The first grade didn't happen by accident, so don't let it fall off by accident. Take ownership and accountability for the grade you caused. Apply the same routine, the same preparation as you did for the first. Your performance will always regulate at your belief level, but because you have raised your level of expectation in yourself, you perform at a whole new level.

NOTES

E14

Four Phases of Goal Assimilation
Breaking Down the Process

OVERVIEW

There are four distinctive, yet fluid, phases in the goal assimilation process. Each one has its place and cannot be passed over if we truly desire to reach our goals.

OBJECTIVES

By the end of this unit, I will understand:

- the value of creating clear and accurate goals.

- current reality as it pertains to creating the necessary discontent.

- I want to be open to finding the information I need to achieve my goals.

- the necessary willingness to change I must have within me.

Don't give up on your goal. Change your habits and attitudes.

LouTice

KEY CONCEPTS

Assimilate/Assimilation: The incorporating of an idea or thought into the subconscious; the absorption or process of incorporating something external into one's body or cognitive processes; making new visions a part of our lives; e.g., one learns and can behaviorally manifest mastery of fundamental mathematical processes.

Attitude: A consciously held belief or opinion; easiest to visualize if we picture ourselves leaning toward those things we like (positive) and away from those things we dislike (negative).

Belief: An emotional acceptance of a proposition, statement, or doctrine.

Expectation: The prospect of a future embodiment of an abstract idea; an anticipation.

Goal(s): A sought end that may be actual and objective, or internal, subjective and operational; conceived future; distal goals are end-results, targets; proximal goals are near-term means to the end-result.

Habit: A learned act; a pattern of activity that has, through repetition, become automatic, fixed, and easily and effortlessly carried out.

NOTES

Write down your ideas, observations and insights as you work through this unit. Date your entries.

REFLECTIVE QUESTIONS

1. Am I struggling to come up with a clear picture of my goals? Why? (not spending enough time with goal-setting; holding myself accountable)

2. Here is a list of at least ten strengths, character traits, personality attributes or behaviors that I am good at:

3. In what areas of my life have I learned to laugh at myself, and not let it bother me or hold me back?

EXERCISE: Finding A Good Coach

Who might I seek out as a coach – someone who will help me see through my scotomas?

	WHO CAN I SEEK OUT AS A COACH?
With Academic matters?	
With Professional matters?	
With Health matters?	
With Spiritual matters?	
With Financial matters?	

EXERCISE: Accountability Partners

Often, it is easier to maintain and sustain ourselves, on our way to our goals, if we have someone who can support our efforts and "has our back" – and we can do the same for them. In the following activity, find someone to partner with – it may be a classmate or colleague – and set a schedule that works for both of you, to help each other reach your goals.

• How many days a week do we intend to meet/talk?

• At what time and for how long?

• What exactly do we intend to discuss?

    o Our affirmations?

    o Habit changes?

    o Attitude or Belief changes?

EXAMPLE CALENDAR AND AGENDA

• We agree to do our affirmations prior to the call.

• Call will last 15 minutes

• Discuss which affirmations give each of us desire and passion to fulfill. Discuss specific tasks we intend to start.

• Are there affirmations that don't seem to be working and why?

	Sun	Mon	Tues	Wed	Thurs	Fri	Sat
Example		7:00 AM	7:00 AM	7:00 AM	7:00 AM	7:00 AM	

SUMMARY: Fundamentals
THE GOAL

It's all about replacement pictures in our mind. The more vivid the image, the more we become discontent with our current image, or current reality as it is right now. The stronger the image, the greater the motivation to achieve it.

Research from Richard Davidson, D. C. Jackson, and Ned H. Kalin, reveals, from a neurological standpoint, that what keeps us moving toward our goals in life comes down to the mind's ability to remind us of how satisfied we'll feel when we accomplish those things. This is a capacity residing in the circuitry between the amygdala, where the brain stores the emotions associated with memories, and the left prefrontal lobe, just behind the forehead, which is the brain's executive center.

Furthermore, as Daniel Goleman, Richard Boyatzis, and Annie Mckee support, all motivators share a common neural pathway – passion for doing the work necessary to achieve the goal. At the brain level, circuits linked to the left prefrontal cortex pump out a steady stream of good feeling as we do our work. At the same time, left prefrontal-based brain circuits perform another motivational favor: They quiet the feelings of frustration or worry that might discourage us from continuing.

To assimilate a goal means we have a clear picture of the outcome, wrapped in positive, inspiring emotions. The more vivid the image, the greater the support from our brain to make it happen.

SELF-AWARENESS

We need to become self-aware of our current reality, our starting point in relationship to the goal, our expected outcome. Some goals will be more tangible, like attendance, studying, completing assignments, grades, and graduation. Others are more intangible, like developing our soft skills, emotional intelligence abilities, or creating better relationships. Either way, whether the goal is easy to picture or a little harder, we need to be as accurate and as honest as possible about our current reality in relationship to our expected outcome.

From Daniel Goleman and his team, self-awareness means having a deep understanding of one's emotions, as well as one's strengths and limitations, values and motives. People with strong self-awareness are realistic. They are neither overly self-critical nor naively hopeful. Rather, they are honest with themselves about themselves. And, they are honest about themselves with others, even to the point of being able to laugh at themselves. Because the decisions of self-aware people mesh with their values, they more often find the work required on the way to their goals as energizing.

INSIGHT

We often are limited by our own perceptions of the world around us – what we think we see. Read the following statement very carefully. It is very important that you understand the statement before we proceed.

```
FINISHED  FILES  ARE
THE  RESULT  OF  YEARS
OF  SCIENTIFIC  STUDY
COMBINED  WITH  THE
EXPERIENCE  OF  MANY
YEARS OF EXPERTS.
```

What you just experienced was the perception of what you read in that statement. The accuracy of our perceptions can be one of the most limiting factors in the goal attainment process. Read the statement again. This time, please be sure to read it even more carefully. Make sure you truly grasp the concept in the statement. And to make certain you are concentrating, please count the number of the letter F you see in the statement. Here is it again.

```
FINISHED  FILES  ARE
THE  RESULT  OF  YEARS
OF  SCIENTIFIC  STUDY
COMBINED  WITH  THE
EXPERIENCE  OF  MANY
YEARS OF EXPERTS.
```

So how many did you see? 2, 3, 5, 7? Let's look again.

```
(F)INISHED  (F)ILES  ARE
THE  RESULT  O(F)  YEARS
O(F)  SCIENTI(F)IC  STUDY
COMBINED  WITH  THE
EXPERIENCE  O(F) MANY
YEARS O(F) EXPERTS.
```

Amazing! What you just experienced is known as a scotoma. It is a Greek word for blindness. A scotoma occurs when information is available, but you just don't perceive it. Even though you looked right at the statement with the intent of counting all the F's, a couple, if not several, didn't get through.

CHANGE OR ADJUSTMENT

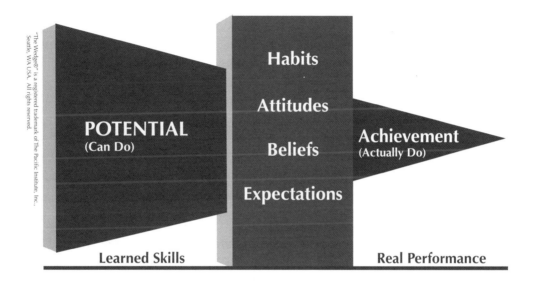

The left side above represents our potential; the right side is the release of our potential. In between are our habits, attitudes, beliefs, and expectations (HABEs). We have spent our lifetime assimilating our HABEs through our perceptions of the world around us. However, many of our HABEs have been assimilated by accident, not by intent.

When we set a goal and begin the assimilation process of making that goal a reality, a vital phase includes the changes and adjustments we are willing to make to achieve our goals. In order to make that manageable, we focus specifically on changes or adjustments to our HABEs. What about my habits, attitudes or current beliefs would I need to consider changing or adjusting in order to get what it is that I expect of myself? Please consider habits, attitudes, beliefs and expectations as a formula, or a strategy toward goal achievement. They provide us with a game plan for challenging previously held perceptions, negative emotions or truths that have been holding us. They provide a framework for specific changes in our actions or thoughts so we can begin operating closer to our true potential.

SUMMARY: Application

Using the example of the Finished Files statement from this segment, let's apply the phases of goal attainment to what you experienced.

GOAL

The ultimate goal was to count the number of letter F's. This was very specific, accurate, and hopefully it gave you a very clear picture of the expectation. But maybe it wasn't. The initial instructions may have had you so focused on understanding the statement that you had a big scotoma to counting the F's. Or you may have dismissed it as irrelevant or secondary compared to the initial instruction. That's entirely fair. Sometimes we can get caught up in distractions on the way to the real goal. Or when coaching, teaching, parenting, or managing, we unintentionally confuse people as to the real goal, which is why clarity and a clear picture are so essential.

SELF-AWARENESS

You probably didn't bother asking yourself, "Where is my current reality, my starting point in relationship to the goal of counting the F's." In other words, you didn't think about how your HABEs or past conditioning might hold you back in your pursuit of the goal (counting all the F's). However, if you got the wrong number of F's, you didn't succeed in achieving the goal, which you were fully capable of doing. It's easy to see why this phase is important to the process.

In the English language, some words are phonetically irregular. They don't sound like they are spelled. We learn to recognize them on sight and assimilate the proper pronunciation of the word. The letter F in the word OF is pronounced as if it were spelled O-V. Through a lifetime of practice and repetition, we assimilated the V sound in place of the F sound. We developed a scotoma, a blind spot, to the actual letter F in the word. This prevented you from the full release of your potential.

INSIGHT

If you didn't happen to see all seven F's the first time counting through the statement, and had to be shown by a classmate or facilitator, you may have initially disagreed or doubted their findings. You may have felt a little embarrassed or foolish when you realized that they were right, thinking, "How could I be so stupid?" Ultimately, you did realize the goal because you were open to the coaching, teaching, mentoring from others or the illustration in the segment to help you release potential. Only because you were willing to consider that you might have a scotoma were you then able to see it differently.

CHANGES OR ADJUSTMENTS

Finally, how did changes or adjustments to the habits, attitudes, or beliefs allow you to reach your goal? In situations where you are capable and have the potential, like with your education, when you have that feeling of "I just can't get it," get in the new habit of asking yourself, "Where might my HABEs or past conditioning be holding me back?"

By seeing through the pronunciation of the word OF – relying automatically upon sight through years of practice and repetition – the letter F came screaming through your scotoma as if it were magic. It wasn't magic. It was getting around a HABE that may have served you well in the past. In this instance, it stood in the way of your goal.

Keep in mind, the phases are fluid. They may not appear in step by step fashion. Rather they are interchangeable pieces of the roadmap on your journey to achieving your goals.

NOTES

EL5

Motivation In-Depth
Inside Me or Outside Me?

OVERVIEW

The brain has spent its lifetime striving to be more efficient, creating pathways that keep us as we "are". Now, we want to challenge and change those pathways, in order to reach our goals. Motivation, both internal and external, becomes the key to staying focused on the end results we want.

OBJECTIVES

By the end of this unit, I will understand:

- extrinsic, or external, motivation is limited in its effectiveness.

- I am more effective when I can provide my own motivation from within.

*We will be stronger and more effective
when we turn on our own motivation from within.*

LouTice

KEY CONCEPTS

Accountable/Accountability: Responsible; answerable for an outcome.

Coercive Motivation: A drive based on fear and/or authority; a have-to.

Constructive Motivation: A positive and free-flowing drive on a want-to basis.

Extrinsic: coming from the outside; not inherent or essential.

Fear: An emotional state in the presence or anticipation of a dangerous or noxious stimulus; an internal subjective experience that is often physically manifested.

Intrinsic: by its very nature, belonging to a thought, idea, goal; necessary.

Or Else: Implicit threat for failure to act according to dictates.

Push-Push Back: When one is pushed, one unconsciously pushes back.

NOTES

Write down your ideas, observations and insights as you work through this unit. Date your entries.

REFLECTIVE QUESTIONS

1. In the decisions I make, am I more motivated by what I stand to lose (to avoid punishment) or by what I stand to gain (reward)?

2. Based on my response to the first question, why do I think this is so?

3. Looking at the most significant people in my life, do they seem to be motivated more by what they stand to lose (to avoid punishment) or by what they stand to gain (reward)?

4. How does this affect how I approach or incentivize people closest to me?

EXERCISE: MY MOTIVATION: Inside Me or Outside Me? – Part 1

What is my present motivation toward completing the tasks that are important in my life right now? Am I intrinsically motivated to get the task completed? Is it because of fear or value? Or am I extrinsically motivated to get the task completed? Is this for a reward or to avoid punishment?

Please fill in the appropriate column below that best describes your motivation with regard to the tasks relevant to your life right now.

| | INTRINSIC? | | EXTRINSIC? | |
RELEVANT TASKS RIGHT NOW	FEAR	PERSONAL VALUE	AVOID PUNISHMENT	REWARD
Attending class				
Doing my school work				
Going to my job				
Parenting				
Being in a significant relationship				
Paying bills				
Saving money				
Cleaning the house				
Preparing meals for myself and others				
Taking my children or siblings to their activities				

Inside Me or Outside Me? – Part 2

Looking at this table, what internal changes can I make to move from Fear to Value?

With those tasks I am doing strictly for external motivation, how can I see them from a more internal – personal pay value – point of view?

SUMMARY: Fundamentals

It should be pretty clear to you that change is not only possible, it is probable, if we choose to change. Through neuroplasticity, we know that our brain is not stone, but more like clay. We can shape it as we aspire to be more, do more, have more and take ourselves closer to our potential in all areas of our lives.

In order to accomplish the changes we expect in our lives, we need to pull on our soft skills, our emotional intelligence abilities. Nothing is greater in this process than motivation. It reminds us of the reasons why we want to change and generates the desire and the passion to keep moving forward. We go where we have the potential to be, rather than settling for where we already are.

Early on, humans had basic requirements for food, shelter, safety and survival. Motivation served us very well because until they are satisfied, we keep going until they are. We are not going to be interested or motivated to do much else. Survival will come first.

As we became more civilized and basic needs were readily met for many, we could adjust our motivation to take us farther. Since we were not worried about having our basic needs met, we aspired to acquire more and improve our standard of living. This gave rise to a next level of motivation, driven by rewards or punishment.

Motivation to avoid punishment. When I was a kid, I may not have wanted to clean my room, but if I didn't, I wasn't allowed to go out and play with my friends. So, I cleaned my room. As an adult, I may not want to pay taxes, but I don't want to go to jail. So, I pay taxes. Motivation to avoid punishment is not ideal, but can be effective in certain circumstances. However, many of us don't enjoy being "motivated" by such negative incentives. It's hard to keep people around us motivated simply because they don't want to be punished. And it's hard to motivate ourselves if we only don't want to be punished.

Motivation by Reward. Our motivation to do a task, perform a function or complete a job could be incentivized. If I am paid, get some type of bonus or reward or perk for doing the job, then I will get it done.

And as we developed into a more sophisticated society, it took money and resources to be able to live a certain way so we responded pretty favorably to a reward system. But what happens when we begin squabbling over the rewards? What do we do when my view of the reward is different than yours? Or what if there really aren't rewards from the outside world to incentivize us? For example, what if I aspire to be a better spouse, a better father, be a better employee, leader, manager, or coach, volunteer more in the community, or help a neighbor? It's harder to tie those to external rewards.

There are inherent, lasting problems to both punishment and reward systems when motivation outside of us isn't sufficient. We need to turn on motivation from within. Extrinsic motivation is artificial and typically not useful for very long. Intrinsic motivation, which is the internal drive and energy released from inside of us, is much more of a long-term solution. External motivation can help, especially in the short-term. But our long-term answer is in our intrinsic motivation.

One type of intrinsic motivation is based on fear. The other is based on something that we value. It is something that we want, that we would like to do, that we love to do.

The intrinsic motivation based on fear is similar to the extrinsic motivation of punishment. The difference is it's self-imposed. It is called coercive motivation. When we are being coerced, the key words are "I have to," and "or else." This mindset is very limiting. As we push ourselves, we push back. We don't like being bullied by someone else, so we sure don't like being bullied by ourselves.

The other type of intrinsic motivation is constructive, by seeing the value. It is why we want to, like to, choose to. We need to figure out why we want to do it. All of our goals must be set on a "want to, choose to, like it, love it, it's my idea" basis, or we are going to rely on extrinsic motivation not intrinsic.

It's easy to remember: When we feel pushed, we push back. We need to have enough self-awareness that when we are forcing ourselves to do something, we can step back. We remind ourselves why we choose to do it, what benefit there is for us and for our family.

When the reward is the activity itself – learning, acquiring new skills, or simply doing our best – there are no shortcuts. It's easy to stay focused and keep going. When we begin to live our lives on a "want to, choose to, like it, love it" basis, we stop forcing ourselves to do things. Surprisingly, we become more accountable and more responsible for our own good and the good of those around us.

NOTES

Imagine, as a group, we discuss running a marathon nine months from now. That's 26.2 miles or 42.2 kilometers. Since many of us may not have an interest in even considering the thought, we will add an incentive. For example, let's say there is an additional $100,000 for the successful completion of the marathon, and it must be within 3-1/2 hours. That works out to a pace of an eight-minute mile, or a five-minute kilometer. Now maybe the money, and the vision of what that amount of money could do for you, has peaked your interest.

If you remember the segment about motivation, the $100,000 is clearly an extrinsic (outside) motivator. It's a reward for the successful completion of the task. Each of us would need to decide if the reward is enticing enough to motivate us for the next nine months of rigorous training. The money is a carrot, an obvious enticement, but not enough on its own. Each of us would need to decide if we can actually see ourselves completing such a task. Do we see ourselves as an active participant in accomplishing the goal of running the marathon in under 3-1/2 hours?

If I don't see myself running it and I'm not playing in it, then regardless of the money (or the amount of money, for that matter – it could be $1,000,000) why try? And even if I do decide to train, I find it really hard to find the drive, energy, desire, and willingness to continually put forth the effort in pursuit of the goal, day after day. I might give it a try in the short term, but I have no real commitment, because, ultimately, I don't see myself accomplishing it. Before long, I simply let go of the goal.

But if I really see how that $100,000 can change my life, or change the life of someone I care about who is in real need, I begin to turn on intrinsic motivators, like how good I will feel and look when I accomplish such a feat. The more vivid that picture is, the more willing I am to do the work necessary in pursuit of the goal.

I start refining and clarifying the picture in my mind. My affirmations might be:

- *I am debt-free and stress-free because my education and my car are paid in full with the $100,000 I earned by completing my first marathon in under 3-1/2 hours.*

- *Exercising, training, and running are exhilarating to me. With each stride, I get one step closer to that $100,000 pile of cash!*

- *It feels incredible and makes me want to train even harder every time my friends tell me that I look great!*

Remember, the affirmation, the picture of what you intend, is not the end result. It is the means to get you the end result. As we work the process of assimilating the new picture – a marathon in under 3:30 with $100,000 to dry my sweat – over and over, our brain creates the drive and energy to start training. It finds the creativity and problem-solving to fit our training into an already busy life. It finds the commitment and accountability not only to train, but also to take care of all the other responsibilities that we have. Just because we are in training doesn't mean that we give up every other responsibility we have. No, we are smart enough and good enough to do it all. We invent the how as we proceed.

We begin to change habits of exercising, of eating, of how we spend our leisure time, and spend time with our family and friends. We begin to balance our schedule differently by multi-tasking, searching for people who can help us and coach us, as well as share their experiences with us. The more we affirm, the more progress we make, the greater the influence we have on our attitude. As we work the habits and see progress toward our goal, we begin to look forward to training and the work necessary to ready ourselves for the marathon. As we progress further, we begin to truly believe, because we see ourselves accomplishing the goal we have assimilated. It has become the new me and the new you. The new truth is that we have the potential. We are capable. We are able. We just need to release it.

This curriculum has been delivered with one goal in mind: the release of human potential. We have a lot more control over our lives than we often consider. We cannot control the world around us, but we can control the world inside of us – how we think, what we expect of ourselves, what we intend to have, be, change, or do.

Please replace the example of the marathon with graduation, the job you want, the career you want, or the relationships you want. You don't need to throw yourself into them. You need to grow yourself into them. Begin with the end in mind and let your brain create the way. Honestly, your brain craves the challenge. You wouldn't have enrolled in the first place if there wasn't at least of piece of you that wants all that your education can provide for you.

> *I am living the life that I deserve, working in the career that I intend, and fruitfully providing for myself and my family because I am a graduate of _____ with a degree in _____ and applying my new skills to the fullest of my potential.*

I offer that affirmation as a template for you to modify and make your own. Please don't be satisfied by setting the goal. Be satisfied by the assimilation and the accomplishment of the goal.

The TPSC MAS Pre-and Post-Inventory is designed as a self-assessment to take before beginning, and after completing, this curriculum.

Read each statement carefully. Circle the response that best fits your judgement at the moment:

- SA = Strongly Agree

- A = Agree

- MA = Mildly Agree

- MD = Mildly Disagree

- D = Disagree

- SD = Strong Disagree

There are no right or wrong answers to the assessment. This is simply your perceptions of the questions being asked.

You are encouraged to take the pre-assessment before beginning Section 2, the Core of the curriculum. This provides you with a baseline from which to measure your growth. When you have completed this course, take the post-assessment, found at the end of Section 3 – the Extended Learning units.

By taking the five to eight minutes to complete the assessment, you have the opportunity to self-assess your perceptions of what you have learned from the concepts in this curriculum.

TPSC MAS Inventory Pre-Assessment

Please read each statement and circle the response that most accurately describes your beliefs and/or feelings.

		Strongly Agree	Agree	Mildly Agree	Mildly Disagree	Disagree	Strongly Disagree
1.	When I enter a new situation, I typically see others as smarter than me.	SA	A	MA	MD	D	SD
2.	My past successes are due to luck.	SA	A	MA	MD	D	SD
3.	In order to achieve a goal, I need to know how I intend to make it happen when I start.	SA	A	MA	MD	D	SD
4.	When I get a good grade it is because I caused it.	SA	A	MA	MD	D	SD
5.	I have complete control of my attitude.	SA	A	MA	MD	D	SD
6.	I am accountable for the goals I set.	SA	A	MA	MD	D	SD
7.	Outside events have a great impact on my life.	SA	A	MA	MD	D	SD
8.	When I am "stuck in my ways," there is no changing me.	SA	A	MA	MD	D	SD
9.	My past successes are because of me.	SA	A	MA	MD	D	SD
10.	When I achieve a goal, it is because I was fortunate.	SA	A	MA	MD	D	SD
11.	I know how my self-talk impacts my attitude.	SA	A	MA	MD	D	SD
12.	I am responsible for my own beliefs.	SA	A	MA	MD	D	SD
13.	My happiness is increased when my goals are met.	SA	A	MA	MD	D	SD
14.	Goal setting is a waste of time.	SA	A	MA	MD	D	SD
15.	It is next to impossible for me to change habits that I have had over most of my lifetime.	SA	A	MA	MD	D	SD
16.	I know how to set goals.	SA	A	MA	MD	D	SD
17.	When I do the work, I can do well on most any assignment.	SA	A	MA	MD	D	SD
18.	I can "turn off" my self talk when it's negative.	SA	A	MA	MD	D	SD
19.	I know how to control my own self-talk	SA	A	MA	MD	D	SD
20.	Good things happen to me because I cause them.	SA	A	MA	MD	D	SD
21.	I have limited control over making changes in me.	SA	A	MA	MD	D	SD
22.	When I set my goals, I get a vivid picture of what I intend.	SA	A	MA	MD	D	SD
23.	I typically need others to solve my problems.	SA	A	MA	MD	D	SD
24.	Despite the attitudes of others around me, I decide my own attitude.	SA	A	MA	MD	D	SD
25.	I know how my self-talk impacts my feelings.	SA	A	MA	MD	D	SD
26.	I let negative past experiences influence my current decisions.	SA	A	MA	MD	D	SD
27.	I know the feeling of wanting something so badly that I can "taste" it.	SA	A	MA	MD	D	SD
28.	It is my choice to be whatever I want to be in life.	SA	A	MA	MD	D	SD
29.	I know how to set goals so that they will become reality.	SA	A	MA	MD	D	SD
30.	When I believe I can do something, I do it.	SA	A	MA	MD	D	SD
31.	If I get a poor grade on a test, it is mostly because of factors outside of my control.	SA	A	MA	MD	D	SD

32.	I let negative opinions from others affect me.	SA	A	MA	MD	D	SD
33.	When I fail to achieve a goal, it is my own fault.	SA	A	MA	MD	D	SD
34.	My negative self-talk leads to negative actions toward others.	SA	A	MA	MD	D	SD
35	I am accountable for my own actions regardless of the situation.	SA	A	MA	MD	D	SD
36.	I typically picture what I want before I get it.	SA	A	MA	MD	D	SD
37.	When I set my mind to it, I make things happen.	SA	A	MA	MD	D	SD
38.	When I don't get support from others, I often give up on my goals.	SA	A	MA	MD	D	SD
39.	Changing a habit is up to me.	SA	A	MA	MD	D	SD
40.	I give up on my goals at some point, because I realize I am not capable.	SA	A	MA	MD	D	SD
41.	Due to past negative experiences, I don't have high expectations of doing well in my courses.	SA	A	MA	MD	D	SD
42.	Writing down my goals is a regular event for me.	SA	A	MA	MD	D	SD
43.	My current study habits are good enough to cause the grades I expect.	SA	A	MA	MD	D	SD
44.	I often picture or imagine what it will look like when I achieve my goals.	SA	A	MA	MD	D	SD
45.	Attending or Logging into my class is an important daily routine.	SA	A	MA	MD	D	SD
46.	I often think about what it will feel like when I accomplish my goals.	SA	A	MA	MD	D	SD
47.	Becoming comfortable in a new situation is within my control.	SA	A	MA	MD	D	SD
48.	When I make up my mind, I cannot be deterred.	SA	A	MA	MD	D	SD
49.	When a task is difficult for me, I tend to quit.	SA	A	MA	MD	D	SD
50.	When I feel out of place, I look to get out as fast as I can.	SA	A	MA	MD	D	SD
51.	When I want something, I make it happen.	SA	A	MA	MD	D	SD
52.	My attitude and the achievement of my goals are not related.	SA	A	MA	MD	D	SD
53.	It is not possible to change a belief.	SA	A	MA	MD	D	SD
54.	I am quick to find excuses when I give up on a goal.	SA	A	MA	MD	D	SD
55.	Most of my current responsibilities are things I choose to do.	SA	A	MA	MD	D	SD
56.	I review my goals on a daily basis.	SA	A	MA	MD	D	SD
57.	When I succeed, it is mostly because of me.	SA	A	MA	MD	D	SD
58.	I have accepted others' opinions of me as truth; they are currently holding me back.	SA	A	MA	MD	D	SD
59.	When I fail, it is typically due to factors outside of my control.	SA	A	MA	MD	D	SD
60.	I have experienced the feeling of having a goal become a part of me.	SA	A	MA	MD	D	SD

Assessment developed by Dr. Scott Fitzgibbon and Dr. Joe Pace

Programs of The Pacific Institute are based on current, highly credible education verified by the most valid, reliable research available.

The Pacific Institute maintains continuing relationships with a number of distinguished human development and social learning theory researchers. We do this to ensure that we are current on important findings related to thought patterns and belief systems – findings that are crucial to our clients. Prominent among these widely respected researchers are the following:

DR. ALBERT BANDURA

Dr. Bandura is the David Starr Jordan Professor of Social Science in Psychology at Stanford University and one of the most frequently cited psychologists in the world. In a recent ranking of the 100 most eminent psychologists of the 20th Century, Dr. Bandura came in fourth, behind B. F. Skinner, Jean Piaget and Sigmund Freud. He is author of countless articles on a wide range of issues in psychology, as well as seven books, including *Principles of Behavior Modification, Social Learning Theory, Social Foundations of Thought and Action,* and *Self-Efficacy: The Exercise of Control.*

Dr. Bandura has been a keynote speaker at The Pacific Institute's International Conference on several occasions. He has also spent many hours with Lou Tice and key Pacific Institute staff informally discussing the relevance of his work on individual and collective efficacy to our education. These discussions have focused on how efficacy is developed, and how perceived high efficacy changes behavior, concepts central to all programs of The Pacific Institute, including *Thought Patterns for a Successful Career®.*

DR. MARTIN E.P. SELIGMAN

Dr. Seligman is Professor of Psychology and Director of Clinical Training at the University of Pennsylvania, where he holds the Kogod Term Professor chair. He is a prolific writer and internationally recognized scholar and researcher. Throughout his career, he has conducted extensive research with grants from the National Institute of Mental Health, the National Institute on Aging, the National Science Foundation, the Guggenheim Foundation, and the MacArthur Foundation. His book, *Learned Optimism: How to Change Your Mind and Your Life,* and his latest work, *What You Can Change and What You Can't,* have received rave reviews. Dr. Seligman has also served as President of the American Psychological Association.

Dr. Seligman's theories of learned helplessness and learned optimism have contributed a great deal to our understanding of human thought and behavior. The Seligman Attributional Style Questionnaire (SASQ) is a widely used tool that measures levels of optimism/pessimism. Dr. Seligman's visits to The Pacific Institute, his keynote presentation at our International Conference, and the time he has spent with Lou Tice at the Tice Ranch, have served to verify and strengthen the conceptual foundation of our curriculum.

DR. GARY LATHAM

Dr. Latham holds the Secretary of State Chair, Faculty of Management, at the University of Toronto. His expertise is in personal and organizational goal-setting and performance appraisal/compensation systems and is well acquainted with The Pacific Institute's curriculum. His latest book, coauthored with Kenneth N. Wexley and published in 1994, is entitled *Increasing Productivity Through Performance Appraisal,* a recent edition of an earlier book of the same title. Dr. Latham was elected President of the Canadian Psychological Association in 1999.

Dr. Latham has consulted with Lou Tice and has addressed The Pacific Institute's staff and clients on numerous occasions, primarily concerning practical applications of the scientific principles of goal-setting, feedback, and performance improvement. He is an outspoken and enthusiastic advocate of our educational processes, and has been a speaker at several International Conferences.

DR. DAVID MATSUMOTO

Dr. Matsumoto is currently an associate professor in the Department of Psychology and Director of the Intercultural and Emotion Research Laboratory at San Francisco State University. His books and monographs include *Culture and Diversity: A World of Differences* (in preparation) and *People: Psychology from a Cultural Perspective.* He is also preparing a video presentation entitled *Culture and Diversity: A World of Differences.* He is the author of more than 50 articles and related symposia presentations throughout the world. As a prior keynote speaker at our International Conference, Dr. Matsumoto consults with The Pacific Institute on matters of cultural diversity – with particular focus on how culture influences behavior and how to manage cultural diversity within organizations.

LEON FESTINGER

In 1954, Leon Festinger developed a concept he called "Cognitive Dissonance." He used it to explain the discomfort he observed in human test subjects when they held two conflicting thoughts at the same time. This discomfort was observed to cause some action: the subject either moved toward one thought or the other. Both thoughts could not be held at the same time.

Rather than see this as a negative situation, Lou takes the idea of cognitive dissonance and uses it as a springboard to create positive change and growth. Since change requires some form of movement, we intentionally create cognitive dissonance in an area where we wish to grow. We make the picture of where we want to be so bright and vivid, that we move toward it, thereby returning harmony.

DR. VIKTOR FRANKL

Distinguished philosopher and author of several books on purpose in life, including *Man's Search for Meaning.* In this book, Dr. Frankl, a concentration camp survivor, relates that the men and women who were best able to survive the terrible physical and psychological deprivation were those who were determined to stay alive because of some reason bigger than themselves. In some cases it was their families. In other cases, it was important work they wanted to continue. And in some instances, it was the services and support they were providing for fellow prisoners.

RICHARD GREGORY

Distinguished psychologist and author of numerous publications. His area of expertise is the cognitive process, especially the relationship between perception and intelligence.

According to the dictionary, intelligence is the capacity for learning and understanding.

Gregory once told Lou that intelligence is simply the "art of guessing correctly." Anything we can do to improve our guesswork is going to make us more intelligent.

DR. WILDER PENFIELD

A cognitive scientist, and author of *Speech and Brain Mechanisms.* During exploratory surgery on a conscious epilepsy patient, with a portion of the skull removed, Dr. Penfield noticed that as he touched the temporal cortex of the patient's brain, the patient relived an experience that had happened years before. As they did further experiments, Dr. Penfield discovered that the information, the individual's version of the experience, was stored in the temporal cortex – never to be lost, never to be forgotten.

NORBERT WIENER

"Founding Father" of the computer, and co-author of the book, *Differential Space, Quantum Systems and Prediction.* Wiener coined the phrase, "Garbage in – Garbage out," in relation to data entered into the computer "brain." Simply put, if you put wrong information into a computer, you cannot get anything but wrong information out of it.

The same thing applies to the human mind. If we accept incorrect information about ourselves into our minds, then we are operating, and making decisions, with incorrect information. We must be careful to accept only correct information, and disregard the incorrect.

On Cognitive Theory and Research applicable to The Pacific Institute's services.

GENERAL

Ashton & Webb (1986) *Making a Difference: Teacher Efficacy and Student Achievement.* Monogram. White Plains, NY: Longman.

Bandura, A. (1986) S*ocial Foundations of Thought and Action: A Social Cognitive Theory.* Englewood Cliffs, NJ: Prentice Hall.

Bandura, A. (1988, Dec) "Organizational Applications of Social Cognitive Theory." *Australian Journal of Management Review,* (Vol. 13, 2, 275-302). The University of New South Wales.

Bandura, A. (1989) "Human Agency in Social Cognitive Theory." *American Psychologist,* (Vol. 44, No. 9, 1175-1184). The American Psychological Association, Inc.

Bandura, A. (1991) "Self Efficacy Mechanism in Psychological Activation and Health Promoting Behavior." *Neurology of Learning Emotion and Affect.* (J. Madden, IV, Ed. 229-270) New York: Raven Press.

Bandura, A. (1991) "Self-Regulation of Motivation through Anticipatory and Self-Regulatory Mechanisms." In R.A. Dienstbiere (Ed.), *Perspectives on Motivation: Nebraska Symposium on Motivation* (Vol. 38, 69-164). Lincoln: University of Nebraska Press.

Bandura, A. (1994) "Self-Efficacy." *Encyclopedia of Human Behavior.* (Vol. 4) Academic Press.

Bandura, A. (1997) *Self-Efficacy. The Exercise of Control.* Freeman, New York, N.Y.

Bandura, A. (1997) *Self-Efficacy in Changing Societies.* Cambridge University Press.

Bandura, A. (2001) "Special Cognitive Theory: An Agentic Perspective." *Annual Review of Psychology.* (52: 1 to 26)

Bandura, A., Barbaranelli, C., Caprara, V., and Pastorelli, C. (2001) "Self-Efficacy Beliefs as Shapers of Children's Aspirations and Career Trajectories." *Child Development,* January/February (Vol. 12, 187-206)

Bandura, A., Caprara, V. and Zsolnai, L. (2001) "Corporate Transgressions Through Moral Disengagement." *Journal of Human Values,* 6.1

Bandura, A. (2004) "Health Promotion by Social-Cognitive Theory." *Health Education and Behavior.* (Vol. 31, 143-164)

Bandura, A. (2006) *Psychological Modeling: Conflicting Theories.* Aldine Transaction.

Barling, J. & Abel, M. (1983) "Self-Efficacy Beliefs and Performance." *Cognitive Theory and Research.* (Vol 7, 265-272).

Barling, J. & Beattie, R. (1983) "Self-Efficacy Beliefs and Sales Performance." *Journal of Organizational Behavior Management.* (Vol. 5, 41-51).

Begley, Sharon (2007) *Train Your Mind, Change Your Brain: How a New Science Reveals Our Extraordinary Potential to Transform Ourselves,* Ballantine Books/Random House Publishing Group, New York

Dembo & Gibson (1984) "Teacher Efficacy." *Journal of Educational Psychology.* (Vol. 76, 569-582).

Dotz, Tom, Hoobyar, Tom and Sanders, Susan (2013) *NLP: The Essential Guide to Neuro-Linguistic Programming,* Harper Collins Publishers, New York

Dotz, Tom, Hoobyar, Tom and Sanders, Susan (1994) *NLP Comprehensive* (1994), Harper Collins Publishers, New York

Duhigg, Charles (2012) *The Power of Habit: Why We Do What We Do in Life and Business.* Random House.

Dweck, Carol Ph.D. (2006) *Mindset: The New Psychology of Success,* Ballantine Books/Random House Publishing Group, New York

Evers, Dr. Anne Marie (2011) *Affirmations Your Passport to Happiness - 8th edition,* Affirmations International Publishing Company, N. Vancouver, BC Canada

Fogel Steven Jay and Rosin, Mark Bruce (2014) *Your Mind Is What Your Brain Does for a Living: Learn How to Make It Work for You,* Greenleaf Book Group Press, Austin, TX

Gardner, H. (1985) "The Mind's New Science." *In A History of The Cognitive Revolution.* New York: Basic Books.

Goleman, Daniel, Boyatzis, Richard and McKee, Anne (2013) *Primal Leadership, With a New Preface by the Authors: Unleashing the Power of Emotional Intelligence* (2013), Harvard Business School Publishing, Boston, MA

Goleman, D. (1995) *Emotional Intelligence.* New York, N.Y., Bantam Books

Goleman, Daniel (1996) *Vital Lies, Simple Truths: The Psychology of Self-Deception.* Simon and Schuster.

Goleman, Daniel (2000) *Working with Emotional Intelligence.* Bantam.

Goleman, Daniel, Boyatzis, Richard E. and McKee, Annie (2004) *Primal Leadership: Learning to Lead with Emotional Intelligence.* Harvard Business Review.

Goleman, Daniel (2006) *Emotional Intelligence: 10th Anniversary Edition; Why It Can Matter More Than IQ.* Bantam.

Goleman, Daniel (2007) *Social Intelligence: The New Science of Human Relationships.* Bantam.

Goleman, Daniel (2011) *Leadership: The Power of Emotional Intelligence.* More Than Sound.

Goleman, Daniel (2011)*The Brain and Emotional Intelligence: New Insights.* More Than Sound.

Goleman, Daniel and Davidson, Richard (2012) T*raining the Brain: Cultivating Emotional Skills.* More Than Sound.

Kaku, Michio Ph.D. (2014) *The Future of the Mind: The Scientific Quest to Understand, Enhance, and Empower the Mind,* Doubleday/Random House LLC, New York.

Mahoney, M. (1978) *Cognition and Behavior Modification.* Cambridge: Ballinger.

Merzenich, Michael Ph.D. (2013) Soft-Wired: How the New Science of Brain Plasticity Can Change your Life, Parnassus Publishing, LLC, San Francisco, CA

Pink, Daniel H. (2009) *Drive: The Surprising Truth About What Motivates Us,* Riverhead Books, New York

Robbins, Daniel (2014) *Emotional Intelligence: The Genius Guide to Maximizing Your Emotional Intelligence - Master Your Emotions, Thoughts, and Communication Skills,* Copyright Globalized Healing LLC

Ungerleider, Steven (1996) *Mental Training for Peak Performance: Top Athletes Reveal the Mind Exercises They Use to Excel,* Rodale Books, Emmaus, PA

CLINICAL APPLICATIONS

Beck, A. (1979) *Cognitive Therapy and Emotional Disorders.* New York: New York Anniversary Library.

Beck, A. (1991) "Cognitive Therapy: A Thirty Years Retrospective." *American Psychologist.* (Vol. 46, No. 4, 368-375).

Beck, A., Emery, G., & Greenberg, R. *Anxiety Disorders and Phobias: A Cognitive Perspective.* New York: Basic Books.

Beck, A., Rush, J., Shaw, B., & Emery, G. (1979) *Cognitive Therapy of Depression.* New York: Guilford Press.

Ellis, H. (1975) *A New Guide to Rational Living.* North Hollywood, CA: Wilshire Books.

Niemark, J. (1987) "The Power of Positive Thinkers." Reprinted from *Success Magazine,* September 1987.

Rush, J., Beck, A., eds. (1988) "Cognitive Therapy." in Francis, A and Hales, R., eds. *Review of Psychiatry.* (Vol. 7). Washington, DC: American Psychiatric Press.

Seligman, Martin, E.P. (1990) *Learned Optimism.* New York: Pocket Books (Simon & Schuster).

Seligman, Martin E. P., Maier, Steven F. and Peterson, Christopher (1995) *Learned Helplessness: A Theory for the Age of Personal Control.* Oxford University Press.

Seligman, Martin E. P. (2003) *Authentic Happiness: Using the New Positive Psychology to Realize Your Potential for Lasting Fulfillment.* Atria Books.

Seligman, Martin E. P. and Peterson, Christopher (2004) *Character Strengths and Virtues: A Handbook and Classification.* Oxford University Press.

Seligman, Martin E. P., Linley, Alex P. and Joseph, Stephen (2004) *Positive Psychology in Practice.* Wiley.

Seligman, Martin E. P. (2006) *Learned Optimism: How to Change Your Mind and Your Life.* Vintage.

Seligman, Martin E. P. (2007) *The Optimistic Child: A Proven Program to Safeguard Children Against Depression and Build Lifelong Resilience.* Mariner Books.

Seligman, Martin E. P. (2007) *What You Can Change and What You Can't: The Complete Guide to Successful Self-Improvement.* Vintage.

Seligman, Martin E. P. (2012) *Flourish: A Visionary New Understanding of Happiness and Well-Being.* Atria Books.

GOAL-SETTING – PERFORMANCE EVALUATION

Latham, G.P. & Wexley, K.N. (1994) *Increasing Productivity Through Performance Appraisal,* 2nd Edition. Reading, Massachusetts: Addison- Wesley Publishing Company.

Latham, Gary P., Mealiea, Laird W. (1995) *Skills for Managerial Success: Theory, Experience, and Practice.* Richard D Irwin.

Latham, Gary P. and Wexley, Kenneth N. (2001) *Developing and Training Human Resources in Organizations.* Prentice Hall.

Latham, Gary P. (2011) *Becoming the Evidence-Based Manager: Making the Science of Management Work for You.* Nicholas Brealey Publishing.

Latham, Gary P. (2011) *Work Motivation: History, Theory, Research, and Practice.* SAGE Publications.

Latham, Gary P. and Locke, Edwin A. (2012) *New Developments in Goal Setting and Task Performance.* Routledge Academic.

Latham, Gary P., Ford, Robert C. and Berrios, Jose A. (2012) *HR at Your Service: Lessons from Benchmark Service Organizations.* Society for Human Resources Management.

Latham, Gary P., Salas, Eduardo, Tannenbaum, Scott and Cohen, Deborah (2013) *Developing and Enhancing Teamwork in Organizations: Evidence-based Best Practices and Guidelines.* Jossey-Bass.

Locke, E.A., & Latham, G.P. (1984) *Goal Setting: A Motivational Technique that Works.* Englewood Cliffs, NJ: Prentice-Hall.

PUBLICATIONS WHICH ARE OF SIGNIFICANT VALUE TO THE PACIFIC INSTITUTE

Bennis, Warren. (1994) *On Becoming A Leader,* Perseus Publication.

Greenwald, Tony. (1995) *Implicit Social Cognition: Attitudes, Self Esteem and Stereotypes Through Social Support Training.* Psychological Review (102) 4-27.

Levin, Henry (1995) "Accomplishments of Accelerated Schools." National Center for Accelerated Schools Project, Stanford.

Marlatt. G. Alan (1992) "Substance Abuse: Implications of a Biopsychosocial Model for Prevention Treatment and Relapse Prevention." Psychopharmacology.

Smoll, Frank (1993) "Enhancement of Children's Self Esteem." *Journal of Applied Psychology.*

Zigler, E. (1993) "Using Research and Theory to Justify and Inform Head Start Expansion." Social Policy Report, S.R.C.D. (Vol. VII #2).

WEB ARTICLES AS REFERENCES

5 Employee Qualities on Every Employer's Wish List, US News & World Report
http://money.usnews.com/money/blogs/outside-voices-careers/2013/09/10/5-employee-qualities-on-every-employers-wish-list

Top Five Personality Traits Employers Hire Most. Forbes.
http://www.forbes.com/sites/meghancasserly/2012/10/04/top-five-personality-traits-employers-hire-most/

Career Attraction Become the Perfect Job Applicant: 15 Traits Employers Look for When Hiring. Ken Sundheim.
http://www.careerattraction.com/become-the-perfect-job-applicant-15-traits-employers-look-for-when-hiring/

8 Traits Employers Really Want in You
http://www.glassdoor.com/blog/8-traits-employers/

Top 10 Reasons Employers Want to Hire You. Rachel Zupek, CareerBuilder.com writer
http://www.careerbuilder.com/Article/CB-1353-Getting-Hired-Top-10-Reasons-Employers-Want-to-Hire-You/

O*Net Resource Center
http://www.onetcenter.org/

National Association of Colleges and Employers
https://www.naceweb.org/

Block, Peter. (2003) *The Answer to How Is Yes: Acting on What Matters.* San Francisco, CA: Berrett-Koehler.

Bosworth, Michael T. (1995) *Solution Selling: Creating Buyers in Difficult Selling Markets.* Burr Ridge, IL: Irwin Professional Publishing.

Bradford, David L., and Allan R. Cohen (1984) *Managing for Excellence: the Guide to Developing High Performance in Contemporary Organizations.* New York: Wiley.

Carnegie, Dale (1982) *How to Win Friends and Influence People.* New York: Pocket.

Carroll, Pete, Yogi Roth, and Kristoffer A. Garin (2010) *Win Forever: Live, Work, and Play like a Champion.* New York: Portfolio.

Collins, James C. (2001) *Good to Great: Why Some Companies Make the Leap--and Others Don't.* New York, NY: Harper Business.

Collins, James C., and Jerry I. Porras (1994) *Built to Last: Successful Habits of Visionary Companies.* New York: Harper Business.

Friedman, Thomas L. (2007) *The World Is Flat: a Brief History of the Twenty-first Century.* New York: Picador/Farrar, Straus and Giroux.

Gladwell, Malcolm (2002) *The Tipping Point: How Little Things Can Make a Big Difference.* Boston: Little, Brown.

Greenberg, Edward S. (2010) *Turbulence: Boeing and the State of American Workers and Managers.* New Haven, Conn.: Yale UP.

Heath, Chip, and Dan Heath. (2007) *Made to Stick: Why Some Ideas Survive and Others Die.* New York: Random House.

Kotter, John P. (2008) *Leading Change.* Boston, Mass: Harvard Business School.

Kotter, John P., and Dan S. Cohen (2002) *The Heart of Change: Real-life Stories of How People Change Their Organizations.* Boston, MA: Harvard Business School.

Kotter, John P., and James L. Heskett (1992) *Corporate Culture and Performance.* New York: Free.

Lipton, Bruce H. (2005) *The Biology of Belief: Unleashing the Power of Consciousness, Matter and Miracles.* Santa Rosa, CA: Mountain of Love/Elite.

McCormack, Mark H. (1984) W*hat They Don't Teach You at Harvard Business School.* Toronto: Bantam.

Mandingo, Og (1983) *The Greatest Salesman in the World.* Bantam.

Nussbaum, Bruce (2013) *Creative Intelligence: Harnessing the Power to Create, Connect, and Inspire.* Harper Business.

Pink, Daniel H. (2006) *A Whole New Mind: Why Right-brainers Will Rule the Future.* New York: Riverhead.

Rath, Tom (2007) *Strengthsfinder 2.0.* New York, NY: Gallup.

Rath, Tom, and Barry Conchie (2009) *Strengths Based Leadership: Great Leaders, Teams, and Why People Follow.* New York: Gallup.

Ryan, Kathleen, and Daniel K. Oestreich (1991) *Driving Fear out of the Workplace: How to Overcome the Invisible Barriers to Quality, Productivity, and Innovation.* San Francisco: Jossey-Bass.

Silverstein, Sam. (2010) *No More Excuses: the Five Accountabilities for Personal and Organizational Growth.* Hoboken, NJ: John Wiley & Sons.

Spitzer, Robert J. (2000) *The Spirit of Leadership: Optimizing Creativity and Change in Organizations.* Provo, UT: Executive Excellence Publishing.

Tice, Lou (1995 rev. 2005) *Smart Talk for Achieving Your Potential: 5 Steps to Get You from Here to There.* Seattle, WA: Pacific Institute Publishing

Tice, Lou, Edited by Glenn Terrell (2005) *Cultures of Excellence: Models of Constructive Leadership and Organizational Performance.* Pacific Institute Publishing.

Tice, Lou, and Joyce Quick (1997) *Personal Coaching for Results.* Nashville: T. Nelson.

Tough, Paul (2013) *How Children Succeed: Grit, Curiosity, and the Hidden Power of Character.* Houghton Mifflin Harcourt.

Updegraff, Robert Rawls. (1916) *Obvious Adams: the Story of a Successful Business Man.* New York: Harper & Brothers.